本书系重庆大学研究生教育
教学改革重点项目"硕博共
享双师型国际合作课程建
设"（cqu230210）、重庆市
研究生交叉学科导师团队"语
言、认知与智能计算"建设
项目（ydstd1923）和重庆
大学中央高校基本科研业务
费项目"大中小学校一体化
外语教育研究与实践平台"
（2023CDJSKPT06）的阶段性
研究成果。

U0461148

《面向学习的测评：
一种系统的方法》百问

辜向东　汪　咏　李玉龙 / 编 著

重庆大学出版社

图书在版编目（CIP）数据

《面向学习的测评：一种系统的方法》百问 / 辜向东，
汪咏，李玉龙编著.--重庆：重庆大学出版社，2023.12
ISBN 978-7-5689-3910-2

Ⅰ.①面… Ⅱ.①辜… ②汪… ③李… Ⅲ.①教学评
估 Ⅳ.①G420

中国国家版本馆CIP数据核字（2023）第095718号

《面向学习的测评：一种系统的方法》百问

辜向东 汪 咏 李玉龙 编著
策划编辑：安 娜
责任编辑：安 娜 书籍设计：叶抒扬
责任校对：邹 忌 责任印制：赵 晟

重庆大学出版社出版发行
出版人：陈晓阳
社址：重庆市沙坪坝区大学城西路 21 号
邮编：401331
电话：（023）88617190 88617185（中小学）
传真：（023）88617186 88617166
网址：http://www.cqup.com.cn
邮箱：fxk@cqup.com.cn（营销中心）
全国新华书店经销
重庆市国丰印务有限责任公司印刷
*
开本：720mm×1020mm 1/16 印张：15.5 字数：305 千
2023 年 12 月第 1 版 2023 年 12 月第 1 次印刷
ISBN 978-7-5689-3910-2 定价：68.00 元

《面向学习的测评：一种系统的方法》（*Learning Oriented Assessment: A Systemic Approach*）一书 2016 年由剑桥大学出版社出版，2019 年由外语教学与研究出版社引进国内。本书是剑桥"语言测试研究"系列丛书中的一本。两位作者分别是剑桥大学英语考评部（Cambridge English Language Assessment，简称考评部）的 Neil Jones 和 Nick Saville。

书中提出了语言测评领域一种新的测评范式——面向学习的测评，英文名称为 Learning Oriented Assessment，作者特别强调，为了有别于其他学者对面向学习的测评的研究，本书的正标题首字母需要大写，简称 LOA。该模式具有系统性和生态性，是将终结性评价（summative assessment）和形成性评价（formative assessment）相结合的有益探索。

关于 LOA，考评部官网的解释如下：LOA 的提出是为了从传统测评方式中探索出一种新的测评范式，该范式注重信度和效度，首要目标是促进学生的语言学习。LOA 的系统性表现为它强调多种测评方式在多个层面以不同形式加以运转，既包括在宏观层面上设置教育目标和成就评价标准，又包括在微观层面上促进个人在课堂内外进行学习互动。LOA 强调所有层面的测评方式都能够并且应该保障学习的有效性和评价的可靠性。LOA 基于对定量测量维度和定性个性化方法的功能划分，界定了测评和教学的互补关系，把教师放在创造学习环境的中心位置，把正式测评（formal assessment）引入学习环境中以取得积极的影响。

本书提到了 LOA 六个方面的研发背景。

（1）基于测试反拨效应（washback），即外部测评（external assessment）对学校和课堂环境下的教与学的影响。

自 20 世纪 80 年代以来，受交际法（communicative approach）对教学和测评的影响，学者们开始对反拨效应产生浓厚兴趣。当时虽然很多教师认为测评会对教学产生积极的影响，测评的内容和形式对课堂教学具有积极的引导作用，但是高风险考试也有阻碍学习的一面，例如，很多学生总结的应试技巧影响了考试的效度。事实上，测评的影响不仅涉及学生的课堂学习，而且会延伸到社会的各个方面，例如，测评会影响教育政策的制定和整个教育生态系统。考评部一直致力于研究测评如何促进正式教育环境下的教学，并使测评对课堂教学产生积极的反拨效应。随着测试反拨效应的研究范围不断扩大，考评部思考的测试反拨效应的维度也由课堂和学校层面上升到整个社会层面。

（2）基于测评"二分法"对立的传统。

一直以来，一提到测评，很多学者就会想到几组对立面：终结性评价和形成性评价，标准化评价（standardised assessment）和课堂评价（classroom assessment），以评测学（assessment of learning）和以评促学（assessment for learning）。每组的前者都具备以下特征：在学习结束时实施；基于某项教学大纲或者理论模型；设计基于信度和效度的统筹考虑；作为一种判断，经常与"评分"挂钩，是对过往学习成果的"回头看"。与之相反，每组的后者则具备以下特征：具有不间断性；是对学习者不断变化的需求的回应；注重交流、支持和发展；被贴上缺乏"信度"和"效度"的标签；目的是"向前看"引导学生前进。几组对立面的前者和后者看起来互相对立，实际上可以相辅相成、相互融合，共同促进学习，这是考评部研究的焦点，即让看似对立的测评整合在一起，服务学生的学习。

（3）基于《欧洲语言共同参考框架》（The Common European Framework of Reference for Languages，简称《欧框》）的确立。

在欧洲，从 1989 年至 2010 年，测评改革小组（Assessment Reform Group）深入研究了以评促学，以提高教育水平、提升教学效果。这个目标反映到测评中就是研发新的量表，以更加准确地评估学习者的学习情况，构建解释性框架，将学习成果报告给利益相关者。在这一需求下，《欧框》应运而生。《欧框》独立于任何形式的语言测评，它是对不同程度的语言水平所作的系列描述，包括在任何一个等级上的人对于该语言应该有怎样的运用能力。就 LOA 而言，依托于一个解释性框架至关重要，《欧框》的诞生为 LOA 的提出奠定了理论基础与框架。

（4）基于对"学习"和"二语习得"的理解。

建构主义（constructivism）强调学习者的主动性，认为学习是学习者基于原有的知识和经验生成意义和建构理解的过程，而这一过程常常是在社会文化互动中完成的。建构主义对教学和学习具有重要的意义，而社会建构主义（social constructivism）则进一步强调学习的社会性和合作性。建构主义，尤其是社会建构主义，让人们深思"学习"的本质，而"二语习得"作为"学习"的一种特例，也需要探讨学习的社会属性，这也促进了 LOA 的研究。

（5）基于对"教育状况改变"的认识。

Dewey（1916）指出，教育的目标是使个体能够继续他们的教育。对于正式教育下的学习者而言，他们要学习的内容不仅仅是课程教学目标要求的知识，更重要的是学习者要学会改善性情和态度，掌握实际的学习技巧，这对于学习者而言意义重大，因为学习是终身的。从建构主义角度而言，如果能够将课程、教学、测评和社会融合在一起去促进学习，那么教育的目的性和连贯性就可以得到保障，课程学习目标的达成和学习者终身学习能力的养成就有实现的可能，而《欧框》的研制就是这种可能的一个范例。基于《欧框》，LOA 致力于培养学生的学习能力，促进其终身学习，力图为教育状况的改变提供新的思路。

（6）基于移动技术的发展。

自 20 世纪中叶以来，信息技术快速发展，移动设备应运而生。在此背景下，人们的信息存储与处理能力以及知识的获取能力显著增强，学习开始与移动设备挂钩。这为 LOA 的提出奠定了技术基础。

本书具有三大特色。

特色一：探索了大规模测试和课堂评价的共性与互补性，更新了读者对测评的理解。大规模测试以其总结性特征，通过对学习者学习成果的判断、描述、记录和报告，来衡量学习者在一段时间内的学习成效。课堂评价具有形成性特征，能够通过教师对学习者的情感、态度和策略的观察、记录和反思来展现学习者的日常表现和进步。LOA 是一种综合性思维，它提供了一种系统性的评估模型，在某种教育背景下的多个层面上运行，并具有不同的表现形式（Jones et al. 2013）。

它既包括宏观层面上制订的教育目标和评价结果，也包括微观层面上个体在教室内外进行的学习互动（Jones 2014）。基于《欧框》，LOA 在宏观层面为外部测试提供交流技巧、主旨、话题、功能、任务等方面的参考，指导外部测试实施，产生成就记录；在微观层面制订 LOA 大纲，指导课堂评价。课堂评价作为内部测评，主要围绕 LOA 活动以获取非正式的成就记录。这些记录和外部测试的成就记录共同为 LOA 提供了促进学习的证据。外部测试的成就记录既要能够诠释《欧框》和 LOA 大纲，又要起到对课程成就的外部终结性测试进行监控的作用。通过将这两种测评结合，借助二者的优势，LOA 可以产生有价值的结果：促进学习，提升测评的解释力度。

特色二：构建了"四个世界"，并将四者以"任务"为驱动形成环状，以服务于"学习"的目的。这"四个世界"为"个人""教育""社会""测评"，分别代表个人认知的发展、课程学习、社会技能和专门语言技能的获取、测评任务的构建。"个人"运用"任务"发展个体的认知；"教育"运用"任务"设计课堂练习、组织正式教学；"社会"运用"任务"评价技能表现；"测评"以"任务"为测量基础。通过"任务"驱动实现了两种方式的"学习"：在现实世界中通过参与"任务"实现自然习得（natural acquisition）和在正式教育环境中通过接受教育实现学习。通过"四个世界"，个人、教育、社会、测评构成了一个连贯的有机体，体现了 LOA 的系统性和生态性。"四个世界"也体现了 LOA 的社会认知性，例如，个人为了获得进入社会所需要的技能，可以通过接受教育获得认知的发展，实现学习的进步。LOA 对学习的诠释体现了教育的本质：学习不只发生在课堂，而应贯穿学习者的一生。

特色三：LOA 的实施设想涵盖了一系列利益相关者，在一定程度上使 LOA 更具可行性和可操作性。LOA 认为，考试机构应该负责制订测试的总体原则；政策制定者对相关政策的批准和实施应起到关键作用；学习者和教师是 LOA 实施的关键参与者，学习者应该积极主动参与到学习中，教师的主要责任是创造良好的学习环境、观察学习过程、反馈学习成效；教育管理者也应该参与到 LOA 中，为 LOA 的实施提供必要的软硬件设施。

总之，本书理论性强，囊括了大量与语言测评相关的议题、原则与实践。语言测评理论及概念涉及项目反应理论（item response theory）、题库、过程描述（processing accounts）、复杂理论（complexity theory）、基于频次的描述

（frequency-based account）等。书中探讨了大规模测试与课堂评价目标和标准的整合问题，提供了 LOA 视域下新时代的课堂评价模式。本书写作体例合理，按照"什么是学习""要学习什么""要测评什么"的思路进行撰写，阐释了 LOA 的基本内容，指出了教师、学习者、测评专家等应该如何利用 LOA 促进教学、学习和测评。每章开头都引用了 Dewey 的观点道破本章主旨，大部分章节结束时都会加以总结，便于读者理解。

本书系统地介绍了剑桥英语视域下的 LOA，对国内读者具有一定的参考价值。为了建构 LOA，本书梳理了 LOA 的研究根源，探讨了学习和语言学习的内容、学习的目标，以及大规模测试和课堂评价在学习中扮演的角色，并把大规模测试与课堂评价加以整合，提出了 LOA 的实施方案。

本书探讨的 LOA，深化了我们对终结性评价和形成性评价二者互补关系的认识，有助于我们理解如何基于这两种测评收集促进学习的证据、提高测评的质量。本书把促进学习的证据分为定性证据（qualitative evidence）和定量证据（quantitative evidence）。定性证据指的是水平维度（horizontal dimension）的日常教学和学习，探讨"如何帮助每位学习者获得进步"；定量证据指的是垂直维度（vertical dimension）的测试，探讨"学生进步了多少"。本书认为水平维度和垂直维度有互补，也有重合：定量证据可以帮助每位学习者鉴定技能水平，定性证据可以帮助学习者获得定量测评体现的学习成果。这种阐释更新了我们对"二元对立"的认识，为我们开展终结性评价和形成性评价的整合研究提供了思路。

本书倡导的 LOA 具有系统性、生态性、社会认知性，有助于我们理解学习的本质，同时有助于外语教师转变教学理念、创新教学方法、实施更加有效的教学与测评。阅读本书，我们会认识到，学习并非简单的"教与学""学与测"，而是一种社会认知行为。学习需要基于行动，在测评"任务"驱动的"交互"中才能更有效地进行；学习需要突破课堂的时空限制，把学习者的认知发展与他们在社会中的发展相统筹，培养让学习者受益终身的性情、态度和技能。这些观点对于国内语言政策的制定、课程大纲的设计、教学内容的组织具有启发意义。

本书一共九章。第一章总体引介 LOA，介绍了全书的编排结构，并着重介绍以"任务"（task）为驱动的四个"世界"——"个人""教育""社会""测评"。

第二章主要探究 LOA 的发展源起，介绍了 LOA 在不同背景下的发展情况，并列举了一些面向学习的方法。第三章至第五章提出了 LOA 涉及的三个基本问题：什么是学习？什么是语言学习？要学习什么？第六章到第八章探讨了大规模测试在学习中的角色和 LOA 在课堂中扮演的角色，以及二者的结合问题。第九章阐述了全面实施 LOA 涉及的问题，如教育政策制定、形成性评价实践的经验教训、技术的关键作用等，以及实施 LOA 的大体步骤。

外语教学与研究出版社第 66 期"我来读文献"活动（2020 年 3 月）围绕语言测评展开，由本书导读作者之一辜向东带读。导读分为三个阶段：第一阶段总引；第二阶段专著正文阅读；第三阶段扩展阅读、思考与实践。每个阶段会设置一些建议的思考题，阶段结束的当日晚上集中在线交流与讨论。

第一阶段　总引

阅读内容：

Contents

导读

本专著的两篇英文书评和一篇中文书评

List of tables and figures

Abbreviations

Acknowledgments

Series editors' note

References

Author index

Subject index

第二阶段　专著正文阅读

阅读内容：

Chapter 1　　Learning Oriented Assessment: An overview

Chapter 2　　The roots of Learning Oriented Assessment

Chapter 3　　What is learning?

Chapter 4　　What is language learning?

第三阶段　扩展阅读、思考与实践

扩展阅读内容：

第一阶段第 10—13 思考题中收集的文献

团队收集的关于 LOA 和面向学习的测评的相关文献

参与本次导读活动的有本科生、硕士生、博士生；助教、讲师、副教授、教授；小学教师、中学教师、大学教师；他们有的是语言测试领域的入门者，有的是这个领域的专家或博导。读者群体背景丰富，结合师生交流和辜向东教授的思考，最终确定这期导读的主题为"语言测试专著阅读与科研能力提升"，以实践"To read, write, think and dream"的理念。

本专著共九章，160 页。考虑到读者在上学或工作，时间和精力比较有限，所以计划每两天阅读 1 章。辜向东教授与本专著书评和导读的合作者——贝尔法斯特女王大学在读博士生李玉龙，结合对本专著的理解和相关学术会议上与会者的提问，拟定了一些关于 LOA 的思考题，供阅读时参考。需要特别说明的是，这些思考题并没有标准或特定参考答案，目的是方便读者一起交流讨论，分享彼此的阅读与思考，碰撞出更多思想的火花。为保持讨论话语的风格与特色，本书参考答案多以中英文混合的形式出现。

编者感谢外研社第 66 期"我来读文献"活动的所有参与者，特别致谢以下导读活动的参与者（按姓氏字母顺序排列）：陈彩霞、陈艳清、陈泽涵、邓超群、胡瑜、李明珠、李天宇、梁沛东、刘源、罗拾霞、罗顺、彭红、宋京蔚、甜甜、王浩、王永利、王志芳、魏藏锋、谢颖怡、叶雯琳、尹开兰、翟娜、张海会、郑蝉金、曾妍妮、曾长萍等，还有外研社段长城团队，尤其是李海萍对导读活动的组织、互动答疑（见附录）。特别感谢原著第二作者 Nick Saville 参与导读第二和第三阶段的线上答疑。

图目录
List of Figures

表目录
List of Tables

目 录
Contents

总引
Introduction

第一章　面向学习的测评：概览
Chapter 1　Learning Oriented Assessment: An overview

状？"We could do better." 思考我们作为个体怎样可以做得更好。

第二章　面向学习的测评源起
Chapter 2　The roots of Learning Oriented Assessment

第三章　什么是学习？
Chapter 3　What is learning？

第四章　什么是语言学习？
Chapter 4　What is language learning？

1. 请翻译本章开始前引用的杜威的话（There's all the difference in the

第五章　要学习什么?
Chapter 5　What is to be learned?

第六章　大规模测评在学习中的作用
Chapter 6　The role of large-scale assessment in learning

assessment，谈谈你对他们此话的理解（Educational assessment must be understood as a social practice, an art as much as a science, a humanistic project with all the challenges this implies）。推荐李筱菊教授的《语言测试科学与艺术》（湖南教育出版社 2001 版）。

5. 请翻译 Messick（1989）对效度的定义："An overall evaluative judgment of the degree to which evidence and theoretical rationales support the adequacy and appropriateness of interpretations and actions based on test scores"（p. 86），并谈谈你对此的理解。

6. 请重读本章对 Weir(2005) Socio-cognitive validity framework 的介绍（pp. 88-89）。推荐阅读本人国家社科基金重点项目申报书"基于证据的大学英语四六级、雅思、托福考试效度对比研究"，并谈谈你的理解与收获。

7. 你赞同大规模测试的四点优势吗（p. 90）？请谈谈你校或你本人是如何使用我国相关的大规模语言测试结果 / 数据的？

8. 请问你是否有认真完整地阅读过相关的教学大纲（如高中的新课标、大学英语课程标准、英语专业本科教学质量国家标准等）？如果没有，请查找阅读，并谈谈你阅读后的收获。

9. 请问你是否认真完整地阅读过我国的大规模英语测试（如高考英语、大学英语四六级考试、英语专业四八级考试、全国硕士研究生入学英语考试等）的考试大纲？如果没有，请查找阅读，并谈谈你阅读后的收获。

10. 请查阅我国大规模语言测试分数解释 / 报道的权威性文献和我国大规模语言测试发展历程的权威性文献，在群里分享并谈谈你的阅读收获。

11. 请查看国内大规模语言测试的官网，并对比国外的大规模语言测试的官网（如雅思、托福考试的官网），对比其异同。

第七章　面向学习的课堂评价
Chapter 7　Learning-oriented assessment in the classroom

1. 请翻译杜威名句（Give the pupils something to do, not something to learn and the doing is of such a nature as to demand thinking; learning naturally results.），并谈谈你对该名句的理解。

2. LOA 课堂的本质是什么？
3. 请谈谈你对 Figure 7.1（p.98）的解读。
4. 请重读 7.6 In summary（pp.104-105）面向学习的课堂特征，对照这些特征反思我们自己的教学实践，看有哪些方面需要改进？
5. 请分享你或者你的老师的课堂测评实践，并结合 Figure 7.1 对这些实践进行自评。

第八章　大规模测评和课堂评价的对接
Chapter 8　Aligning large-scale and classroom assessment

1. 翻译杜威名句（The two limits of every unit of thinking are a perplexed, troubled, or confused situation at the beginning, and a cleared up, unified, resolved situation at the close.）。结合本章内容，谈谈你对此名句的理解。
2. 请再拟一遍本章的目录，从本章论述的五个方面反思与自评你的教、学、测、评实践。
3. 请用 Green(2012) 建议的方法（p.109）分析《中国英语能力等级量表》

第九章　实施面向学习的测评
Chapter 9　Implementing Learning Oriented Assessment

附录
Appendix

could you give us some advice?　　　　　　　　　　　　　

4. 首先感谢辜老师近段时间用心、专业、尽力、无私、热情的指导和分享，我现在特别想问：1）近段时间由于您的团队和各位群友的分享，我们积累了大量的中英文素材，一下子感觉太幸福。但是这么多宝贵的资料，又有些不知道该如何科学合理地阅读才能使这些材料真正地发挥其作用和价值。如何才能使它们不仅仅是一份材料，更是成为我们的知识积累和储备，真正地能为我们的教学和科研服务？关于这一点，您有什么建议？2）您觉得对于青年教师来说，考博是必须的吗？如果不考博，能否通过日常学习来补足？如何来补足？

5. 我是一名入职两年的初中英语教师，教学管理一直让我比较头疼，所以想请教您：1）大班化教学，学校处于城乡接合部，学生的学习主动性和积极性不高，考虑到学生每天有大量的作业和课程，该如何有效地要求学生，进而促进学生学习呢？2）严师出高徒，想跟您请教您平时是如何落实对学生的严格要求的？

6. 请您推荐一些适合非英语专业学生的阅读材料，可以从哪里搜集？比如您提到的CNN，手机App好像下载不了英文版。

7. 1）作为教师，我们在平时的教学中如何去实施测试来辅助教学。在平时的教学中我喜欢用一些小测试，检验学生所学的知识，口头的比较多。现在我们上网课，测试的频率可以比线下多，形式比线下丰富，并且能够快速得到结果的直观呈现。那么我们如何才能对这些结果进行有效的分析和解读？2）您在教学方面做过什么样的测试，哪些测试活动您认为是比较有效的；测试完成后，我们需要做些什么，您能不能跟我们说一说？3）目前我在对学生进行英语专业四级的阅读和完形填空的训练。那么我怎么从英语专业四级测试入手，来进行一些相关的研究呢？

8. 作为一位非测试研究方向的外语教师，需要了解多少相关知识比较有利于实际的英语教学呢？既然已经看了一些相关文献，如果要写测试学或者教学类的学术论文，是不是必须要会用SPSS等软件进行数据分析，投稿才有希望？

总引
Introduction

"目录"补充思考题及作答

1. 第一次读完目录，你有什么困惑？

参考作答 1

阅读《面向学习的测评：一种系统的的方法》的目录之后，存在的困惑主要有以下三点：

（1）第一章的概览没有涵盖后面所有章节的内容，如第二章、第七章、第九章的内容未得到体现；第一章的二级标题 1.5 与第六章从标题上看，标题内容存在一定的对应关系，但不完全对应。

（2）第四章有点突兀，或者说如果抛开此章，本书也是一本很好的教育学专著。当然，语言教学是教育的一个特殊领域。既然如此，本书对语言测试是否同样有用？如果是，是否可以增加有关语言学习，包括自然语言习得 / 测试、二语习得 / 测试方面的介绍？如果是针对教育这个大领域提出 LOA，那又为何只在此章略微提到什么是语言学习？

（3）全书在编排上将 LOA 放到前面来阐述，可以理解是最开始对这个概念进行解释，但是紧接着介绍 what is learning / what is language learning / what is to be learned，从章节题目设置看是与 LOA 不相关的。在此书九个章节中，只有四个章节与 LOA 有直接联系，其余四个章节的内容并不完全是关于 LOA 的，附录中没有一个部分是关于 LOA 的。

参考作答 2

（1）第一章的概览基本涵盖了全书各个章节的内容（除了第一章 LOA 的理论基础和第九章 LOA 的实施），概览二级标题 1.2—1.6 分别对应第三至八章的内容。困惑是既然 1.1 已经说明了本书的架构，为何还要用一章的篇幅来给后面每一章进行说明？为什么不把小节的内容放进相应的章节里？作者有何用意？

（2）本书是 LOA，引入第六章大规模测评在学习中的作用是出于什么目的？另外，目录格式不完全统一。

2. 作者逻辑思路清晰吗？结构上是否存在不足？

参考作答 1

Basically, the author follows a descending thinking route: Chapters 1 and 2 give an overview and the roots of LOA. The rest chapters develop from learning, language learning, learning outcome to large-scale assessment, classroom assessment, a combination of these two and implementation of LOA at last. However, the author devoted too many lengths to topics beyond LOA. In addition, more empirical studies of LOA are needed.

参考作答 2

作者的逻辑是清晰的，大标题环环相扣且部分也和总论对应，小标题也层层递进，基本是先总论述再进行细化，最后总结。从第一章概览，第二章 LOA 的理论基础，到第三章学习，第四章语言学习，第五章学什么，再到第六章大规模测试在学习中的角色，第七章 LOA 在课堂评价中的作用，第八章大规模测试与课堂评价的对接，第九章 LOA 的实施。在学习与测评之间，大规模测试与课堂评价之间架起了一座桥梁。

不足之处：首先，结构上每一章的格式不统一，有的章节没 In Summary 或者用了 In Conclusion；其次对于 LOA 的关注还不够，分散了更多精力写相关的背景（我会更想看到已有、现存的研究）；最后，如果把第二章的内容放到第七章之前，第八章放在第六章后面是否会更好？

参考作答 3

作者逻辑思路是比较清楚的。先是总体介绍，之后再分别阐述每一个主题，最后几乎每一章都有一个总结。

不足之处：首先，书名 a systemic approach，approach 一词在语言教学可指理论性的，也可指具体的方法，我拿到书的第一感觉以为会是比较具体的方法，但是从目录看还是理论指导，导读中也提到了，没有告诉我们如何去实践；其次，有一些章节后面并没有总结。

3. 从目录判断，哪些章节你可能理解上比较困难？

参考作答 1

Chapter 9. This chapter talks about the implementation of LOA. I've seen the status quo, the example of Asset Languages, the rescue means and impacts, but there is little mentioning of LOA implementation steps, principles, and successful empirical studies.

参考作答 2

第六至九章理解上比较困难，因为个人缺少测试相关实践经验。第六章涉及一些测试术语；第八和第九章，个人认为将大规模测试和课堂评价相结合的章节会需要更多的背景知识，将 LOA 应用于实践也需要更深层次的理解。

4. 第一章总引的目录涵盖了后面所有的章节吗?

参考作答 1

No. Chapter 2 The roots of Learning Oriented Assessment, Chapter 6 The role of large-scale assessment in learning, and more importantly, Chapter 9 Implementing LOA are not mentioned.

参考作答 2

没有涵盖所有章节，第二、六和第九章在目录中并没有涉及。

5. 目录中有哪些表述前后不一致?

参考作答 1

（1）第一章二级标题 1.5 The roles of assessment in learning 和第六章一级标题 The role of large-scale assessment in learning 不一致。从标题上看不是完全对应，从标题内容上看又存在一定的联系。

（2）In Summary 和 A Conclusion 表述不一致，比如第一、第三、第四、第五、第六和第七章都以 In summary 结尾，而第九章以 A conclusion 结尾，并且第二章和第八章既没有 In summary，也没有 A conclusion。

参考作答 2

目录中，第一章二级标题 1.6 、第七章二级标题 7.1 和第八章标题三处在指课堂评价时，表述不一致。另外，learning 和 oriented 之间是否有连字符（hyphen）也不一致。

6. 基于 "9.4 Technology to the rescue?" 猜测作者的态度。

参考作答 1

The authors might not be optimistic about LOA implementation for which technology can hardly be a remedy.

参考作答 2

作者认为信息化时代可以很好地帮助我们完成面向学习的测评，本书的理念和现在所倡导的智慧教学理念相似，后者强调以智慧学习为中心。这个问号给人一种作者想要读者去文中找答案的感觉，很吸引人。

参考作答 3

作者对技术能够推动 LOA 的实现打了问号，暗示其不是十分看好技术的作用，存疑。

7. 为什么三个附录有两个是关于 "assessment for learning" 的？

参考作答 1

Perhaps there are few official principles of LOA implementation or effective pedagogy that have been formed and concluded. The principles of assessment for learning implementation can be used for reference.

参考作答 2

为了研究主题的需要，本书主要侧重 learning 这个过程，是针对学习的测评，所以用了两个附录，将测评与学习更紧密地结合。

8. 外研社版为什么没有"List of tables and figures"和"Author index"?

参考作答 1

I've scanned other books introduced by Foreign Language Teaching and Research Press, in which "List of tables and figures" and "Author index" are also not found. There is only "Subject index". I found that most of the original foreign books have list of tables and figures and subject index. I cannot work out other reasons than the book compiling tradition in China. In my view, list of tables and figures is a must, which shows the findings of the research and should be clearly read or referred to by the readers. The author index and subject index have different usages. It's best to present all the three.

参考作答 2

个人猜测也许外研社版觉得以开门见山的方式展开内容更方便阅读，同时这些表格和图表也可以在文中找到，并不影响阅读；也可能是因为 List of tables and figures 和 Subject index 会占相当大的篇幅，不呈现使书籍看起来更简洁。

9. 如果你来写"What is learning？""What is language learning?""What is to be learned?"，你会从哪些方面来写?

参考作答 1

Considering the purpose of assessment, my development of writing might be based on the constructs that will be assessed. For "what is learning", the behaviorism (stimulus-response, reinforcement，etc.), cognitive views (memory, knowledge, metacognition, and problem solving) and constructivism (situation, cooperation, dialog and meaning construction) learning theories and practices might be covered. For "what is language learning", both the lower-level curriculum objectives and higher-order communicative skills will be included. "What's to be learned" perhaps comprises the three learning outcomes of LOA: curriculum content, higher-order outcome and transferable learning skills and dispositions.

参考作答 2

针对"What is learning"部分，先解释 learning 的定义，之后拓展一些 learning 的相关方面；"What is language learning"部分，先阐述语言的相关定义，然后对语言学习进行解释，可以联系二语习得进行拓展，抑或是进行一语习得和二语习得的对比；"What is to be learned"部分，介绍支撑三者发展的理论和研究，三者分别存在什么突出特性，简述三者的异同点，更主要的是将其与 LOA 联系起来。

"导读"补充思考题及参考作答

1. 剑桥大学英语考评部官网有没有定义 LOA？

参考作答

Yes.

The term Learning Oriented Assessment is one of several which have been used in recent years with a similar purpose in mind: to carve out a place for a form of assessment with different priorities and values from those of traditional assessment, with its focus on reliability and validity. Like the classroom-based assessment movement in the US, or the Assessment Reform Group's promotion of formative assessment or Assessment for Learning in the UK, LOA proposes a form of assessment whose primary purpose is to promote learning.

Cambridge English approaches LOA from an assessment specialist perspective, taking a systemic view where assessment operates on multiple levels and takes many forms. It encompasses both the macro level of framing educational goals and evaluating outcomes, and the micro level of individual learning interactions which take place in the classroom or outside it—that is, both formal and informal assessment. The term LOA is chosen to emphasize that all levels of assessment can and should contribute to both the effectiveness of learning and the reliable evaluation of outcomes.

Our conception of LOA reflects an intention to change the traditional relationship of assessment to learning. The Cambridge model sets out to define a complementary relationship with teaching, based on a functional division between the dimensions of quantitative measurement (the domain of assessment expertise), and qualitative individualization of approach to each learner (the domain of teaching expertise). LOA thus foresees a central role for teachers in creating an environment productive of learning, wholly complementary to the role of formal assessment.

An important goal and motivation in developing LOA is to shape the approach taken in situations where Cambridge English exams are adopted at institutional or national level within a programme of educational reform. LOA should serve as a theory of action for introducing formal assessment into a context of learning so as to achieve positive impact.

2. 你是否赞同导读中总结的那些"二分法"异同？还有可以补充的点吗？

参考作答 1

In this book, criterion referenced test and norm referenced test, classroom assessment and large-scale tests, are contradictory pairs, which are put a little bit differently in "导读". The authors also elaborated on proficiency and achievement test, which are not a contradictory pair.

参考作答 2

赞同。导读中的"二分法"分别从过程、种类和作用进行了分类。也可以对评价对象进行分类，如分为教师评价和自我评价 (参照等级量表进行)，也可以按照评价阶段分为学前评价和学后评价，还可以增加"诊断性评价"和"过程性评价"。

3. 导读中总结的特色是本书的特色吗？还有没总结到的特色吗？

参考作答 1

Yes, I think they are the major features of this book. If there is more, perhaps learning-oriented feature, which is also the foundation of the book and LOA. We can refer to Chapters of "What is learning?" "What is language learning?" and "What is to be learned?"

参考作答 2

总结的特色很全面。但是，对我来说，LOA 这个方法提出及其实施本身也应该算是一个特色。

参考作答 3

总结的是本书特色，但是作者聚焦于理论和内容上的一些特色，关于本书结构上的特色未做足够阐释。

4. 你对图 1 和图 2 的理解有困难吗？导读中的阐释清楚吗？

参考作答 1

图 1 对我来说，其实是存在一些理解上的困难的。对基于《欧框》中所表达的宏观和微观层面的理解似乎会有一些模糊；文章中涉及的图有点复杂，作者没有进一步解释，尤其是图中各因素之间的逻辑关系不太清楚。

参考作答 2

图 1 的箭头我觉得有点乱，而且 high-level objectives 和 contents 看起来似乎没有联系；图 2 比较清晰。导读阐述从微观和宏观两方面展开，比较清楚。

参考作答 3

They can be easily understood. The points are elaborated clearly and accurately.

5. 本书是按照"什么是学习""要学习什么""要测评什么"这样的思路来写的吗？为什么？

参考作答 1

The authors follow a sequence from "what is learning？" "what is language learning？" "what is to be learned？" to large-scale assessment, classroom assessment, a combination of these two and implementation of LOA at last. Whenever we talked about assessment, perhaps there should be what, why and how.

参考作答 2

The authors defined learning before the content of learning and assessment in that LOA is based on learning first. Besides, the research is oriented to learning. It seems to be a cycle, learning → LOA → learning. It is necessary for us (researchers, teachers, etc.) to make clear these definitions which may facilitate our learning and teaching.

参考作答 3

是的，各章节的大标题可以体现出作者的写作思路和逻辑。

可能因为本书是 Learning Oriented Assessment，"面向学习的测评"，需要将相关的学习和测试知识先介绍清楚，然后再具体介绍将如何推行。

6. 阅读这篇导读，你得到了什么启发？导读中给你印象最深的地方或一句话是什么？导读还可以从哪些方面进行改进？

参考作答 1

启发：首先，我了解了一本专著的导读结构大概包含哪些方面。其次，导读给了我关于这本专著的一个初步的全面的认识，也让我了解了本书的不足，比如我在阅读目录时，没有发现章节设置不一致的问题。最后，导读提出的几个思考题给了我未来研究方向的一些启发。

导读中印象最深的一句话是：学习需要突破课堂的时空限制，把学习者的认知发展与他们在社会中的发展相统筹，培养让学习者受益终身的性情、态度和技能。

作为一线教师，我在教学实践中总是脱离不了课本内容，无法将语言知识的学习和学生在社会的发展相统筹，没有做到"授之以渔"。或许在了解了 LOA 之后，了解了学生应该学什么以及测评应该测什么之后，就能更好地将课堂延伸出去，让学习贯穿一生。

导读可改进之处：可以用例子来解释图 1 和图 2。

参考作答 2

启发：导读部分给我的感觉像是在写书评，但是它不仅仅是对书中内容的描述，还有总的一些概述，补充说明的一些知识，阐释了特色以及不足。由于这是引进版，所以比较实际地写了对国内读者有何意义。

导读印象最深的一句话："学习不只发生在课堂，而应贯穿学习者的一生。其实除了要学习书本上的知识，也应该不断学习生活中的知识，而这些学习在系统的方法指导下都能获得比想象更好的结果。"

导读可改进之处：个人认为可以把书中的一些理论做一个专门的列表，在读者阅读之前可以先进行大致的了解，更有利于提高兴趣和帮助阅读。

参考作答 3

启发：导读是从宏观角度对一本书进行引介并且要让大家对这本书产生印象，需要将书中最有特色、最核心的内容总结出来并简洁地呈现。

导读印象最深的地方：对导读中两个图的呈现印象很深。因为图表有时候可以承载的信息很多；同时"学习不只发生在课堂，而应贯穿学习者的一生。其实除了要学习书本上的知识，也应该不断学习生活中的知识，而这些学习在系统的方法指导下都能获得比想象更好的结果。"这句话也令我印象深刻。

导读可改进之处：个人认为特色部分可以再精简一点，同时将本书整体不足部分专门列出，会更清楚一些。

7. 如果你来写这篇导读，会怎么写？

参考作答 1

先介绍背景知识，然后进行内容概括，最后对书的特色进行介绍，说明该书的意义。同时会在导读结尾附上涉及的重要理论的讲解，以提高读者阅读兴趣和帮助读者阅读。

参考作答 2

It sets a good example of how to write a book review for its comprehensive covering mentioned above, critical comments and thought-provoking questions at the end.

Book Review 补充思考题与参考作答

1. 相同作者的中文导读(辜向东、李玉龙)和英文书评(李玉龙、辜向东)在内容和写作风格上的相同点和不同点是什么? 为什么相同作者对同一部专著的导读和书评在内容和写作风格上会存在不同?

参考作答 1

（1）内容和写作风格上的相同点：首先中文导读和英文书评就内容上来说，都简洁明了地总括了全书的架构，介绍了书中每一章节所涉及的内容，并提及了应用 LOA 本身的意义。其次，中文导读和英文书评就写作风格来说都比较严谨客观，一般采用总—分的结构，此外章节介绍部分并非堆砌，而有其内在逻辑，作者承上启下，为了说清楚 LOA 的来龙去脉，从 LOA 源起讲到学习以及语言学习，随后涉及国家教育背景下的语言学习以及大规模测试与 LOA 综合模式的构建，最后以应用 LOA 结尾，逻辑清晰不拖沓。

（2）内容和写作风格上的不同点：首先在内容上，中文导读篇幅更长，涉及的内容也更多，不但包含书籍章节信息本身，对为什么研发 LOA，以及 LOA 的理论意义和实践意义都分别做了比较详细的阐述；反观英文书评篇幅短得多，以简洁阐述 LOA 是为了促学这一目的作为大背景引入，随后涉及的也大多是书籍章目信息本身，没有其他解读，信息量也比较有限。其次写作风格上，中文导读注重以问题导入；英文书评囿于篇幅似乎显得平淡。

（3）不同之处的原因：第一是发表的平台不同，中文导读很可能附在书籍之中，起到的作用更像是展示这本书提及的理论意义，而英文书评发表于相关杂志期刊，它必须在有限的篇幅下满足期刊读者的需求，起到的作用更像是展示这本书与其他书籍在细节上的不同；第二是读者群体的区别带来读者关注点的不同，中文导读面向的是中文读者，它必须考虑到很多中国读者实际的科研现状以及教育现实，因为这正是中文读者所关注的，而英文书评面向的读者群体则更有可能来自不同的国别，因此在书评中更重要的是尽可能简洁地报告这本书里的主要内容。

参考作答 2

（1）中文导读的结构：

概述（书名，出版年份，出版社，属于何种系列，作者，本书核心 LOA 及其定义，六大方面的研发背景）、内容简介（分章节简介和突出每章的关键性术语）、本书特色（特色 1-3，加综合。其中重点介绍书中关键图表 LOA 实践模型和"四个世界"）以及本书对国内读者的意义（总结 LOA 的构建过程，"二元互补"理念，社会认知行为下学习与测评的关系），最后是四个思考题。

（2）英文书评的结构：

背景、全书结构介绍、分章节简介（1-2，3-5 分三段介绍，6-8 分三段介绍，9）。本书特色与不足：章节开始时引用美国教育学家杜威的话，对双语环境下如何实施 LOA 考虑不足，最后一段是本书的意义以及推荐的理由。

（3）相同点：都介绍了本书的背景、章节的内容、本书的特色以及不足、意义。不同点：导读更加详细，书评在介绍本书的内容时更加突出"评"。

（4）不同之处的原因：存在不同的原因首先是两种文体的写作目的不同，写作风格也不同。书评更加浓缩，注重评，即评价，突出写作特色，侧重的是 How；而导读更加详细，注重导，即向导，更像"导航"，侧重的是 What。

参考作答 3

（1）相同点：

在内容上，中文导读和英文书评都对整本书进行了分类归纳和总结，并不是逐一介绍每章的内容。如把 Chapters 3-5 放在一起来介绍 learning 这一概念的基本内容；Chapters 6-8 放在一起介绍 assessment 这一概念的基本内容。

在写作风格上，中文导读和英文书评框架结构清晰、语言文字简洁易懂。让读者能够迅速抓住该书的主要内容。读完导读和书评就能够对本书中的关键概念有些印象。总体觉得这本书确实值得去读，关于 LOA 也有很多值得研究的地方。

（2）不同点：

在内容上，中文导读更加清晰。第一部分就对本书的研发背景进行条目式列举，让人一目了然 Why is LOA worth studying? 我还注意到中文导读有这样一句话"作者特别强调，为了有别于其他学者对面向学习的测评的研究，本书的正标题首字母需要大写，简称为 LOA"。

不知道其他的学者在对面向学习的测评进行研究时，他们用的什么提法和概念。"本书的特色"这个部分我很喜欢，把 LOA 的实践模型和以"任务"为中心连接的"四个世界"用图示的形式展示出来，特别好。我第一感觉就是，如果要做这方面的研究，是有原型可以借鉴和参考的。最后一个部分，本书对国内读者的意义，其实也是一种很好的指引作用。对于像我这样测试方面的新手来说，读了这个部分，知道自己应该怎么入门去了解 LOA。最后作者给出了特别值得思考和讨论的问题，其实就是未来做研究可以着手的点。这里的第 3 个问题"如何确保利益相关者，尤其是教师达到 LOA 的要求？"吸引了我。虽然我读的文献不多，但感觉 LOA 是以学生为主的研究，教师在 LOA 中的角色如何，从教师的角度研究，是不是也是一个点？

在写作风格上，就语言本身而言，我感觉中文导读的语言就像一位长者在耳边轻轻地告诉你，带领着你去读这本书的内容：为什么要读，怎么去读，读完了你可以做什么。英文的书评阐述清晰、简洁易懂。

2. 两篇英文书评（Li & Gu, 2018；Cao, 2019）在内容和写作风格上有何异同？导致异同的原因可能是什么？

参考作答 1

Li and Gu (2018) adopt plain and easily accessible language for their book review. Starting with a general summary of the nine chapters, they introduce each chapter with the main idea, the key features, and the supporting claims. At the end of the review, they provide general comments along with a brief critique of the limited scope of the target subjects.

Cao (2019) follows a similar structure, with a summary, an introduction of each chapter and comments and critiques. What distinguishes her writing is the style she adopts and the voices she adds to the introductions. Cao (2019) adopts an exhaustive way of introducing each chapter, including a detailed articulation of the arguments and claims made by the book. She also makes her own comments on the content and even reading suggestions to the readers.

The differences between the two book reviews could attribute to the different positioning of the authors. In their review, Li and Gu (2018) pull themselves out of the narratives. They stay as objective as possible, leaving the space of comment and critique for readers. Cao (2019), on the other hand, is more involved in her review. She introduces her opinions and tries to play a more active role in readers' understanding.

参考作答 2

They are similar in the structure: introduction, contents of each chapter, comments, and recommendation. The major difference of (between) these two lies in the section of comments. Li and Gu (2018) showed slight concern about the reader friendliness of the book. However, Cao (2019) seemed to be more critical and put forward lengths of suggestions on the book's practicality, the social function of assessment, the ambiguity of some concepts and confusion in some figures. The difference may be caused by different understandings of the focus and function of a book review or perhaps just the authors' different writing styles.

参考作答 3

（1）相同点：结构相同（书籍写作背景＋书籍内容＋评论）。

（2）不同点：Li & Gu（2018）：篇幅更短，注重介绍书籍内容本身（多数章节的介绍侧重点在内容布局——作者在这一章做了什么），评论部分稍显不足（主要谈及该书优点）；Cao（2019）：篇幅更长，书籍写作背景部分结合了相关文献，注重提炼作者的核心观点（在介绍章节内容时给出小规模论证，让读者更有获得感），给目标读者提供阅读建议，评论部分较为充实（既谈优点，也说不足）。

（3）原因：相同的原因可能是英文书评的结构大体上是一致的，写作风格也相对类似；不同的原因可能是书评作者自身的写作风格和写作着手的角度不同。

3. 中文导读与中文书评在内容和写作风格上有何异同？导致异同的原因可能是什么？

参考作答 1

（1）相同之处：内容上，导读和书评都包含本专著的背景、内容简介、本书特色和不足之处。写作风格上都很专业和正式，运用术语很多。

（2）不同之处：内容上，导读的每一个部分篇幅长短恰当，对 LOA 的解释和研发背景介绍非常详细，最后单列一个部分谈本专著对国内读者的意义，提出四个问题引导读者去思考。书评的每个部分篇幅长短不一，其中对于内容的介绍非常详细，读起来觉得比导读的内容简介更加翔实细致。但书评中关于本书的特色和不足篇幅较短。书评中，评价的部分应该是重点。

（3）相同可能的原因：内容风格上相同的原因或许是导读和书评应该都能够给读者呈现一个本专著的整体画面，让读者对该专著有一个大体的认识，因此就要有写作背景、主要内容和简单的评价（反思）。

（4）不同可能的原因：导读扮演一个引子的作用，在内容上只是点到即止，并设计思考题，引发读者在阅读正文时不是单纯地去读，而是要在阅读的过程中思考；而书评，是要向读者展示作者对专著的认识和评价，是要体现出作者对专著内容的一个批判性思维，所以在启发性方面不如导读来得强烈。

参考作答 2

They have certain similarities in the major contents of the book. Their styles are differentiated greatly. Li (2018), notwithstanding its easy-to-be-understood, went a little bit far from the original book. The notion of assessment as learning is almost not mentioned in the book, whereas the author just proposed assessment of and for learning repeatedly. His comments on the nature of learning are not a focus but the basis of the book. The Chinese book review by Li and Gu (2019) gave faithful and detailed review of the book contents, appropriate conclusion of its features and shortcomings. What is more, the thought-provoking questions at the end are beneficial for teachers and researchers on assessment.

4. 简评三篇书评各自的特色与不足。

参考作答1

特色：辜向东和李玉龙的导读倾向于以问题导入，从为什么研发，到介绍研发成果，以及成果有什么意义，十分清晰；曹琳琳的书评注重逻辑引领，引导读者去理解原文作者的思路；李亮的书评注重细节介绍，较多地涵盖了书籍本身的细节信息。

不足：辜向东和李玉龙的导读似乎偏抽象，特别是第三节介绍书籍特色时对于图表的阐释；曹琳琳的书评对于细节介绍略微简洁；而李亮的书评则似乎欠缺逻辑的串联。

参考作答2

（1）Li & Gu（2018）特色：简明扼要地介绍书籍内容；不足：对各章节的核心观点介绍不够。

（2）Cao（2019）特色：各章节有核心观点，也有评论；不足：评论部分对书籍的优点阐释不足。

（3）Li（2018）特色："简要评价"部分，作者能结合文献探讨该书的主要特色；不足："内容简介"部分，各段内部句子之间的逻辑关系不是很清楚（部分段落，不能清楚地区分哪些是专著的内容，哪些是书评者的评论）。

参考作答 3

Li and Gu's (2018) book review is objective and reader-friendly. However, there is more space for them to include more critique about the content, structure, and arguments of the book. Some readers may expect in-depth analysis and critical reviews in their writing.

Cao's (2019) book review is comprehensive in terms of introduction of the content, the arguments, and the articulation of her own critique. However, the introduction could be too meticulous for some readers, as key ideas might not be spotted from the first glance.

Li's (2018) book review involves a detailed introduction to the main ideas and arguments of each chapter. However, again, there is also more room for the author to critique the arguments made and the structure designed.

参考作答 4

（1）李亮老师的中文书评分为三部分：先给出背景知识总述；然后再进行内容介绍，其中每一章都给出了该章的总述或是在全篇中的作用，再对内容进行概括；最后对该书进行了简要评价。个人觉得老师提出的三个特点较好（加入了个人关于 LOA 结合社会和学校的一些想法）。如果将内容中每一章介绍的结构统一会更完美（每段第一句简介章节大意，再进行介绍）。

（2）曹老师的书评针对该书内容进行了总述，然后再对每一章进行详细阐述，最后对 LOA 理论模型提出了一些实践性的建议，这个是比较好的一点。阐述也较为详细，使读者能够更好地理解书中的内容。但是如果文章的排版能够再清晰一些，比如把对第一段中第一章的介绍和最后一段中第九章的介绍单独排成一段会更好一些。

（3）辜老师和李老师的书评在介绍内容时分为五个部分进行，这样对读者更为友好，使读者能够更快地理清专著的思路。最后对于本书提出的问题，如果能做出进一步的解答和建议会更好。此外，如果能对本书的特点提出自己大体的评价也会更完美。

5. 综合三篇书评和导读，概括本专著的特色与不足。

参考作答 1

特色：从社会建构主义视角，综合大规模测评与课堂评价的共性和互补性，界定了测评与教学的互补关系，加深了读者对测评的理解；所构建的"四个世界"体现了 LOA 的系统性与生态性；设想了利益相关者，一定程度上有可行性；形成了自己独特的评价体系（assessment for/of/as learning）——LOA 体系；本书每章以名言开头，围绕章节主题，得体贴切；著作结尾提供的三个附录，尤其是前面两个对提高教师测评素养很有启发和帮助。

不足：书中的一些图表较为复杂，缺乏进一步的解释；LOA 实践模型操作起来困难；整体结构上存在一些混乱、不统一的地方。

参考作答 2

Judging from the three book reviews and the contents, the book has a clear structure, with each chapter targeting at a critical topic pertinent to the research and practice of learning-oriented assessment. Here, I will mainly address two aspects of the book of possible improvement.

Firstly, feedback has not been considered as a major factor that determines the success of classroom-based learning-oriented assessment. The book argues that "to generate interactions leading to learning" and "to capture evidence of interaction" are the two major concerns of learning-oriented classroom assessment (Cao, 2019, p. 2; Li & Gu, 2018, p. 498). These two factors are crucial for the implementation of assessment for learning, as they help to design assessment practice that elicits evidence of students' achievement and to make decisions about the next step that further instructs students' learning (Black & Wiliam, 2009). However, the book seems to neglect the importance of feedback, which is defined by Shute (2008, p. 153) as "information communicated to the learner that is intended to modify his or her thinking or behavior to improve learning". As Stobart (2012) argues, feedback is one of the key issues that influence validity in assessment for learning. Without being given appropriate guidance and feedback, students may benefit from the classroom interaction in a limited way.

Secondly, the book has addressed both the issue of alignment between large-scale assessment and classroom learning-oriented assessment and the issue of alignment between learning and assessment. These two issues are essential in language education, as the objective of learning and the evaluation standards should remain in a coherent way to ensure the efficiency of teaching and learning. Without such alignment, all classrooms could end up as what the famous quote says: "the assessment tail always wags the curriculum dog" (Broadfoot, 2007, p. 8; Gardner, 2012, p. 104; Kelly, 2009, p. 148). For the structure of this book, my sense is that there is an absence of the teacher's perspective. Bernstein (2003, p. 156) identified the relationship of curriculum, pedagogy and assessment as the three-message system of any educational setting: curriculum stands for what knowledge should be learnt; pedagogy stands for how knowledge should be transmitted; assessment stands for how learning could be recognised and future learning be informed. The book could give us a more comprehensive perspective of how learning-oriented assessment can be operated in class if addressing how teachers should design their pedagogy aligning with their class curriculum and the current assessment they adopted.

References

Bernstein, B. (2003). *Class, codes and control: Theoretical studies towards a sociology of language.* Routledge.

Black, P., & Wiliam, D. (2009). Developing the theory of formative assessment. *Educational Assessment, Evaluation and Accountability, 21*(1), 5-31.

Broadfoot, P. (2007). *An introduction to assessment.* Continuum.

Cao, L. (2019). Review of the book *Learning Oriented Assessment: A systemic approach* by N. Jones & N. Saville. *TESOL Journal, 10*(3), 1-4.

Gardner, J. (2012). Quality assessment practice. In J. Gardner (Ed.), *Assessment and learning* (2nd ed., pp. 103-122). SAGE.

Kelly, A. V. (2009). *The curriculum: Theory and practice* (6th ed.). SAGE.

Li, Y., & Gu, X. (2018). Review of the book *Learning Oriented Assessment: A systemic approach* by N. Jones & N. Saville. *Innovations in Education and Teaching International, 55*(4), 497-498.

Shute, V. (2008). Focus on formative feedback. *Review of Educational Research, 78*(1), 153-189.

Stobart, G. (2012). Validity in formative assessment. In J. Gardner (Ed.), *Assessment and learning* (2nd ed., pp. 133-146). SAGE.

李亮.《学习导向的评价——系统方法》评价 [J]. 外语测试与教学，2018，32（04）：56-58+63.

参考作答 3

特色：

（1）探索大规模考试和课堂评价的共性和互补性；

（2）构建了"四个世界"，以任务驱动，让四者可以服务于学习；

（3）设想了利益相关者，一定程度上有可行性；

（4）形成了自己独特的评价体系（assessment for/of/as learning），LOA 体系；

（5）内容编排用心，每一章前用杜威的名句引入。

不足：

（1）该模型比较理想化，对于 LOA 具体如何实施，没有给出更加具体的范式或借鉴；

（2）整体结构上存在一些混乱、不统一的地方，容易让人产生疑惑。

参考作答 4

特色：第一，本书打破二分法，又综合起个人、社会、学校和评价四个维度，有很大的理论创新意义和实践价值。第二，本书探讨学习的本质，提出了独特的评价体系模型，对我国教育发展有借鉴意义。第三，本书每章以名言开头，结合章节主题，得体贴切。

不足：第一，LOA 没有明确的定义，LOA 在实际操作中可能会遇到很多现实问题，而这些现实问题很有可能在书中找不到答案。第二，各个章节存在写作风格不统一的问题，这有可能给读者阅读带来障碍。第三，章节安排不尽合理，第七章的内容似乎应该放到第八章，而且不仅对 LOA 模型阐述不够详细，还忽视了语言测试的社会功能。因此，本书需要更加合理的编排，以及对某些细节更加详尽的解释。

List of tables and figures 补充思考题与参考作答

1. 为什么专著一般会单列图表目录？

参考作答 1

首先，图表目录概括性强，涵盖的信息量大，单列出来方便读者了解内容；其次，很多图表涵盖了一些重要的方法和理论、框架等内容，单列出来也方便读者了解、查阅，更容易记住（但是给出的图表目录中没有标注页码，如果有页码会更好）。

参考作答 2

单列图表目录的目的是让读者更清楚地看到研究内容、研究重点和研究结果。而且图表一般是按顺序罗列的，所以能够让读者了解到研究的体系和过程。图表目录中出现的标题关键词一般也是书的关键词，能帮助读者很快定位出想获得的信息；甚至根据图表目录，读者可以了解作者要阐述的一些观点和内容，了解不同图表直接交互可能存在的关系。

参考作答 3

The tables and figures are the visual presentation of the essential data of a study, which reflects the development of the research. By scanning through the tables and figures, readers can gain a general picture of the methods and results of the book.

参考作答 4

图表是文字的补充与辅助手段，意味着该部分内容的复杂度或者重要度可通过图表得到更好的呈现，因此图表常具有很大的概括性。单列图表目录可帮助读者更快获取专著中的重点，读者通常可以通过图表获取某个章节或部分的中心内容。

2. 从完整图表目录看，你认为本专著的重点是什么？与前面阅读的专著目录有何不同？

参考作答 1

（1）重点：从图表来看，本专著的重点应该是学习（learning）以及它的"四个世界"，同时通过一些理论来说明 LOA。

（2）不同点：不同之处在于专著目录在表明逻辑关系的同时，还通过术语简略地告诉读者逻辑过程；虽然图表目录也有一定逻辑性，但是总体松散。专著目录覆盖面广，更能体现全书内容；图表则只会在需要的章节才能出现，所以覆盖的内容不全面。

参考作答 2

（1）重点：从图表目录来看本书中的"四个世界"（Four Worlds）似乎是重点，加之对于 LOA 相关的框架（socio-cognitive framework 等）的介绍。

（2）不同点：专著的目录呈现整本书的内容，重视整体性；图表目录侧重介绍重要概念、核心模型、研究实施步骤、研究结果等，代表不同方面，不像专著目录那样存在着总—分的关系，但是图表存在相互联系。

3. 请就每一个图表提出一个思考题。

参考作答 1

1.1 定量评价和定性评价的区分界线适用于母语不同但二语相同的学习者吗？

1.2 为什么只有社会与教育之间存在着相互关系？其他都是单向的联系？

1.3 Assessment 部分的小人为什么挡住了联系的线条，为什么不向下一点？挡住的部分是否有箭头？ Learning 与 social work 为什么是单向的联系？ skills 是否对 constructs 也有反拨作用呢？

1.4 Record of Assessment 没有外向输出的箭头，那它的意义何在？

1.5 LOA Syllabus 为什么只有外向的联系（箭头所指）？

6.1、6.2、7.1：作者为什么选择这些框架？

9.1 为什么实现步骤只包含策略？如何评估结果？

参考作答 2

1.1 为什么横轴与纵轴的交点位于 B1-B2？

1.2 为什么箭头有的双向，有的单向？

1.3 Task 等于 learning 吗？ Task 的定义是什么？

1.4 任何 exam 和 CEFR 都可以对接吗？

1.5 仅有 teacher observation? 有同伴互评吗？

4.1 真的可以 minimize effort in learning 吗？

5.1 真实情景一定严格按箭头自下而上吗？

6.1 Measurement scale 可以准确描述所有 test 的结果吗？

6.2 Context validity 和 scoring validity 之间为什么是双向箭头？

表 7.1 时间间隔的划分依据是什么？

相比图 1.5，图 7.1 删除了 content，是出于什么考虑？

8.1 Subjects 和 constructs 在现实中是完全彼此独立的吗？

9.1 毕竟 LOA 结合了大规模测评，它对 capacity building 的影响相对于课堂评价而言的优势在哪里，如何论证优势确实存在？

参考作答 3

Figure 1.1 In which aspects can large-scale and classroom assessment be complementary?

Figure 1. 2 What are the four worlds? (Already explained)

Figure 1.4 & Figure 1.5 What evidence will the authors provide? How will the authors distinguish macro and micro level evidence?

Figure 6.1. 6.2. 7.1 Why do the authors choose these frameworks? How do these adaptations happen?

Figure 9.1 Why do the implementation steps only contain policy? How do they evaluate the outcome?

Abbreviations 补充思考题与参考作答

1. 为什么专著会单列缩略词目录？

参考作答

（1）方便读者在阅读前对专著中基本的缩略词有一定的了解。缩略词在文中第一次出现是全称，之后直接以缩略的形式出现，单列缩略词目录有助于消除缩略语导致的阅读障碍。

（2）方便读者索引，方便读者在阅读过程中进行查找和对照，突出作者的专业和严谨。

2. 请盖住右边缩略词的全称，勾出左边你熟悉的缩略词，并写出全称，然后检查准确度。

参考作答

　　自己在读的时候这样做过，想挑战一下能记住多少个。第一次记住的不太多，后来发现记住中文意思和对应的英文会有效帮助记忆，记了三遍能记住大部分，但是这应该是短时记忆。

3. 根据你以往的阅读，专著中的缩略词会带给你困扰吗？如果会，是些什么样的困扰？

参考作答

　　会有一些困扰。如果忘记了或者记混了几个缩略词，需要花时间去查找，不仅影响阅读速度，也会打断阅读思路。因为专著本身不一定是读者熟悉的领域，如果使用过多的缩略词，出现频率又不会很高，会加大读者的阅读难度和提高对读者的要求。

4. 请谈谈专著中缩略词使用的利弊，并分享你使用缩略词的经验与策略。

参考作答 1

　　（1）利：文章简洁，去掉一些频繁出现且冗长的表达；制表和制图需简洁明了，当用到长串术语时，缩写能达到制表和制图要求。

　　（2）弊：易遗忘，会增加读者阅读负担，可能会浪费一些时间查找；缩略词可能会重复，即一个缩略词代表多重含义，不同的科研领域有自己的解读，这很有可能使初入科研领域的学生因为知识积累不足而混淆。

（3）经验：使用缩略词时，用注释在醒目的地方写明缩略情况；如果已知此缩略词可代表另外的含义，提醒读者不要混淆；在附录中列出书中使用的所有缩略词。

参考作答 2

When the first time an abbreviation appears, it should be defined. Many journals do not require definitions of abbreviations that are pervasive in the literature, based on the assumption that most readers have already be aware of their meaning. The rule of thumb by The Chicago Manual of Style is that an abbreviation should be used five or more times in a manuscript; if not, then the unabbreviated term should be used. Abbreviation used in the title, abstract, and/or keyword list may be discouraged by journals for the sake of clarity.

Acknowledgements 补充思考题及参考作答

1. 阅读了本专著致谢，你的整体印象是什么？

参考作答 1

首先，一本专著的出版，前期要经过很长一段时间的准备，就像"十年磨一剑"。

其次，出版一本专著，不是凭一己之力，而是在和同行的不断沟通交流中，不断完善。这应该就是建构主义理论下学习的观点，即学习是在社会文化互动中完成的。从致谢的对象可以看出，这本专著的出版不仅凝聚着作者的心血，还有很多人的努力，所以专著的出版不是个人或者仅仅几个人的成果，而是一个团队一起努力的成果。

然后，本书的致谢涉及对象体现了书中理念经过实践的验证和检验，使我开始对阅读有关实施部分充满期待。

最后，致谢涉及的对象也体现出了本书的专业性、系统性和社会性理念。

参考作答 2

The acknowledgements of this book expressed very specific thanks to the people who provided help and described their works in details. Being specific and detailed in thanks shows the authors' recognition and appreciation for the help.

参考作答 3

我从来没有像今天这样认真读过一篇致谢文章，无论是中文致谢还是英文致谢。因为总觉得这个跟我没有很大的关系，都事关别人。但是当我看到下面辜老师列出的思考题（自己尝试写一份致谢）的时候，我先认真读了辜老师公众号里链接的那两篇致谢，之后就对本专著的致谢进行了阅读。

读完致谢，我发现原来一本专著的写作和发表是如此艰难，需要很多人的共同协作，才能最终完成送到读者的手里。本专著的致谢特别真诚。每感谢一个人之后就会在后面附上他们做过的具体工作。从个人到机构等，都非常认真地致谢。在文中运用了一些时间名词 decades，many years，等等，足以证明这本书从编写到出版整个过程的不易。但是，中文专著的致谢很多会增添自己对家人朋友的感谢，而英文的这一篇没有涉及这些。

2. 中英文致谢在写作风格上是否会有差异？为什么？

参考作答 1

存在差异。在语言表达方面，英文致谢出于简洁的目的，并不是每句都写到感谢这两个字，但是中文致谢考虑到重复的语言美，基本每句都会带感谢二字。在致谢顺序方面，大多数中文致谢习惯先表达对机构团体的感谢，其次是对个人的感谢，而英文则相反。

参考作答 2

有差异。个人觉得中文的致谢更多一些程序化的内容，而本书的致谢对象对本书的出版都做了具体的工作。这些人所做的工作从理论到实践，从讨论到阅读，从指导到评价，涉及面很广。

原因：面向的读者群体文化背景不同；写致谢的作者文化背景不同。

3. 请尝试写一份学术致谢（如硕士、博士论文、专著致谢）和 / 或非学术致谢（如邮件、毕业典礼、婚礼致谢）。语言不限，欢迎中英双语。

参考作答 1

Acknowledgements

Here I would like to give my gratitude to all the teachers and friends who have helped me in various respects. First and foremost, I am greatly indebted to my respected teacher, Professor Yongzhong Li, for his valuable instructions, illuminating suggestions and elaborate revision.

Secondly, sincere thanks should go to my teachers, Professor Gretchen Nauman, Professor Xiaoling Cheng, Professor Yuying Li and many excellent teachers who could not be mentioned here. Their proficiency in their own fields, effective teaching methods, and personal charm have deeply impressed and inspired me. Furthermore, during my college years, my faithful friends and amazing schoolmates have given me much emotional support delightfully and generously, which I could never forget.

Finally, my parents and my elder brother have supported me all the way. I am deeply grateful for what they have done for me. Without all those who have helped me, I could not have achieved in writing this thesis.

参考作答 2

首先，非常感谢辜老师一直这么专业和热心，这些优秀品质时刻吸引着我，促使我关注辜老师的公众号，才能够有这么好的机会，来呈现我的思想，表达我的谢意。其次，感谢外研社搭建这么好的平台，使我们有机会接受这种短期的专业学习和指导。再次，群内各位老师的无私奉献精神和乐于分享的美好品质，如兰月秋老师主动和我分享相关材料，翟娜—XJU 第一个分享学习阅读讨论任务，而且一直在坚持分享，还有李天宇老师主动帮助整理群里的分享资料，还有很多其他老师们的精彩分享，这些都是我能够坚持阅读的动力！最后，感谢我自己的坚持和努力！期待经过此次学习，所有人都有所收获！

Series Editors' Note 补充思考题及参考作答

1. 通过阅读 Series Editors' Note 第一段，你预计两位主编接下来会重点写什么？你的预测准确吗？

参考作答 1

The first paragraph states that this book brings together in one place a number of studies of thinking that have been running through developments in language assessment over the past 25 years, so I expected that the editors would give us a history lesson on language assessments, with regard to Learning Oriented Assessment.

Although I have correctly conjectured the general theme that would follow, I missed it in two aspects: Firstly, I did not come up with the washback effect, or the more psychometrics term, validity. Secondly, I did not expect the part on the theories of learning.

参考作答 2

Different strands of thinking and their common interest: assessment should promote successful learning outcomes. Yes, my prediction has been confirmed.

参考作答 3

读了第一段后，我觉得两位主编会介绍之前的关于测试的研究是否得出了结论，即测试是促进还是阻碍成功的学习结果。除此之外，也会介绍这本关于 LOA 的专著如何致力于回答这个问题。

预测不完全准确。读完全书，我觉得两位主编梳理了本研究的一些理论基础、创新性、本想要解决的问题以及所面临的挑战。

2. 请用 50 词左右概括 Series Editors' Note 的主要内容。

参考作答 1

The editors summarize the two lines of works for Learning Oriented Assessment: the washback effect of assessment on instruction, the more expanded notion of impact studies on the social dimension of language testing, and the social cognitive theory on language learning and learning in general.

参考作答 2

Different strands of thinking, e.g., test washback, social impact, assessment approach change, how to learn language and what to learn, share a common learning-oriented interest. Based on the background of assessment reform and development of CEFR, LOA concerns about the language learning and teaching and tries to measure the improvement and outcome systematically and ecologically with the help of technology in the constant changing process.

3. 请标记出 Series Editors' Note 后面参考文献中你阅读过的文献，并就任何一条文献写一段 50 词左右的推介。

参考作答

Spolsky, B. (2004). Review: Continuity and innovation: Revising the Cambridge proficiency in English examination 1913-2002. *ELT Journal, 58*(3), 305-309.

In English-speaking countries and elsewhere publishers have worked hard to produce attractive and profitable books and other materials. Universities and language schools have offered courses and teacher training programmes, and a vast number of websites have offered programs at all levels. In the testing area too, there has been rivalry, but in this case, it has been mainly between two not-for-profit organizations, Educational Testing Service (ETS) in Princeton, New Jersey with its world-wide TOEFL and TOEIC tests, and in Britain the University of Cambridge Local Examination Syndicate (UCLES) with a number of test suites including the Cambridge Proficiency in English Examination. Let's come to the Continuity and Innovation: Revising the Cambridge Proficiency in English Examination 1913-2002.

4. 你认为 Series Editors' Note 后面的参考文献有何突出的特点？为什么？

参考作答 1

参考文献基本上都来自两个系列丛书，SiLT（Studies in Language Testing Series）和 EP（English Profile Studies）。这两个系列都是 Cambridge Assessment English & Cambridge University Press 联合推出的，前者集中在语言测试领域，后者聚焦在《欧框》及其应用。LOA 是基于《欧框》来确立的，为了使两者联系更加紧密所以引用得比较多。

参考作答 2

参考文献主要集中在 Cambridge University Press 的两套丛书：SiLT and English Profile Studies，同时对于 CEFR 的关注也比较多。原因在于本专著作为 SiLT 丛书的一本，编者将之置于剑桥出版的相关系列之中进行阐述，可从参考文献看到整个系列研究的大框架。

首先，参考文献来源主要是 Cambridge: UCLES/ Cambridge University Press 和 Studies in Language Testing。其次，文献名中的 test, washback, CEFR 和 Series Editors' Note 主要内容保持高度一致。

虽然可能欧洲在做测评研究方面比较早，但是参考文献主要集中于某一个地区会不会局限读者对整体的认识？LOA 是不是更适用于欧洲的教育环境？毕竟这是它研究的立足点。所以将 LOA 放在中国教育背景下，结果会怎样？实施运用有很大挑战，需要大量研究。

References 补充思考题及参考作答

1. 参考文献的目的 / 作用是什么？阅读参考文献对你有什么意义 / 帮助？

参考作答 1

参考文献的目的：

（1）保证学术规范，避免抄袭或编造等学术不端行为。

（2）为作者的研究提供支持，读者能从参考文献看出前人前期做了哪些方面的研究，是否全面、深入、及时，并根据参考文献的质量初步判断一篇论文 / 一本专著的学术价值。

（3）为后来的研究者提供帮助。其他对这个研究方向感兴趣的学者可以通过梳理参考文献，迅速找到该领域中的经典著作、权威期刊、高被引学者等，并聚焦学术前沿的热点问题。同时，想要引用作者在文献中所引述的某个观点的学者，也能够通过参考文献找到原始出处，避免二次引用。

参考文献的意义：

参考文献为读者提供了进一步研究的索引，读者可以通过阅读其中提到的文献补全自己所查阅的文献，充实论文写作时的材料，同时也可以在阅读更多文献的过程中修正和完善自己的观点。

参考作答 2

参考文献的目的：

每一篇规范的学术成果（期刊文章、著作、会议论文等）都应该有参考文献，主要是为了：（1）确定文章内容来源，特别是引用等，同时避免出现抄袭等现象；

（2）能够为作者自身的研究留存理论等依据，并且可能会积累较多研究的素材；

（3）为读者提供便利，寻找相关的文献、理论等。

参考文献的意义：

可以帮助读者找到相关文献/作者，对于阅读的专著可以有更深刻的了解，同时联系参考文献，思考之后也有助于自己的研究。

参考作答 3

I think a list of references has three functions. Firstly, using the right and appropriate referencing style can help the writer to avoid plagiarism. Secondly, referencing others' work is giving credit to their efforts or contribution they have made to the field. Thirdly, providing a list of references can help readers to get a better understanding of where different ideas or arguments come from and readers can get access to obtain more detailed information if they need to read the whole piece of work.

I think reading the list of references in a published article or book can help me to identify some items that I have not read but may wish to pursue. In addition, reading the list of references can help me to conduct literature searches on a regular basis, which is essential for me to keep my own research fresh and ahead of what is going on.

参考作答 4

参考文献的目的或作用：

学术写作力求有理有据有创新，而创新不是空中楼阁或者凭空捏造，很多情况下是在前人研究的基础上另辟蹊径。因此在写作时需要表明参考了前人哪些观点，而借此彰显与他人观点的不同又体现创新之所在。因此规范引用文献，使之符合要求是非常重要的，读者可以从文献来判断著作的可读性，这就是参考文献的目的和作用。

阅读参考文献的意义和作用：

（1）查看参考文献目录，判断作者是否引用领域权威专家。

（2）对照参考文献去延伸阅读，判断作者是否歪曲本意。

（3）充实阅读资料，短时间扩大对相关领域专家以及术语关键词的了解，为写作准备素材。

2. 你阅读专著前习惯看参考文献吗？为什么？

参考作答 1

在以写作为目的的阅读中，我常常会在阅读前后看看参考文献。这样可以让我快速了解作者引用了哪些学者的文章；作者看过了哪些文章和专著；参考文献的年份是否体现最新研究热点和趋势；参考文献是否来源于相关领域权威期刊、出版社。

参考作答 2

Yes, I usually read the list of references before I read the content. The reason is that I could make my assumption of the main argument of the article from noticing some important publications of the field. For example, if I read a washback study, the author should cite some influential works in the washback studies, such as Messick (1989), Alderson & Wall (1993), etc.

3. 请列出 15 位左右本专著中引用率高的学者，查阅他们的著述，尤其是最新、最近的著述，做一份文献目录，并分享你在做这项任务的过程中的收获和遇到的困难。

参考作答

（1）Harlen, W.

最近著述：

Harlen, W. (2013). A rather circular look at effective primary science practices. *Studies in Science Education, 49*(1), 93-98.

（2）Dewey, J.

最近著述：

[1] Dewey, J. (2007). *Experience and education.* Macmillan. (Last edited by Simon and Schuster, 1st ed., 1938)

[2] Dewey, J. (2005). *How we think, experience and education* (2nd edition). People's Education Press.

（3）Broadfoot, P.

最近著述：

[1] Broadfoot, P. (2017). Time to tame the leviathan? Perspectives and possibilities for a new era in assessment. *Assessment in Education: Principles, Policy and Practice, 24*(3), 415-423.

[2] Timmis, S., Broadfoot, P., Sutherland, R., & Oldfield, A. (2016). Rethinking assessment in a digital age: opportunities, challenges and risks. *British Educational Research Journal, 42*(3), 454-476.

[3] Timmis, S., Oldfield, A., Sutherland, R., & Broadfoot, P. (2014). *Exploiting the collaborative potential of technology enhanced assessment in higher education.* University of Bristol Press.

[4] Timmis, S., Broadfoot, P., Sutherland, R., & Oldfield, A. (2014). *Ethical issues in technology enhanced assessment.* University of Bristol Press.

（4）Black, P.

最近著述：

[1] Black, P., & Wiliam, D. (2018). Classroom assessment and pedagogy. *Assessment in Education: Principles, Policy & Practice, 25*(6), 551-575.

[2] Black, P. (2017). Christian beliefs and values in science and religious education: an essay to assist the work of teachers of both subjects. *International Studies in Catholic Education, 9*(2), 206-222.

[3] Black, P. & Wiliam, D. (2010). A pleasant surprise. *Phi Delta Kappan, 92*(1), 47-48.

[4] Black, P., & Wiliam, D. (2010). Inside the black box: Raising standards through classroom assessment. *Phi Delta Kappan, 92*(1), 81-90.

（5）VanPatten, B.

最近著述：

[1] Lichtman, K., & VanPatten, B. (2021). Was Krashen right? Forty years later. *Foreign Language Annals, 54*(2), 283-305.

[2] Lichtman, K., & VanPatten, B. (2021). Krashen forty years later: Final comments. *Foreign Language Annals, 54*(2), 336-340.

[3] VanPatten, B., & Smith, M. (2018). Word-order typology and the acquisition of case marking: A self-paced reading study in Latin as a second language. *Second Language Research, 35*(3), 1-24.

（6）Mislevy, R. J.

最近著述：

[1] Mislevy, R. J. (2019). Advances in measurement and cognition. *The ANNALS of the American Academy of Political and Social Science, 683*(1), 164-182.

[2] Dardick, W. R., & Mislevy, R. J. (2016). Reweighting data in the spirit of Tukey: Using Bayesian posterior probabilities as Rasch residuals for studying Misfit. *Educational and Psychological Measurement, 76*(1), 88-113.

（7）Carless. D.

最近著述：

[1] Carless, D. (2020). Longitudinal perspectives on students' experiences of feedback: a need for teacher-student partnerships. *Higher Education Research and Development, 39*(3), 425-438.

[2] Carless, D. (2015). Exploring learning-oriented assessment processes. *Higher Education, 69*(6), 963-976.

（8）Saville, N.

最近著述：

[1] Saville, N. (2019). How can multilingualism be supported through language education in Europe? *Language Assessment Quarterly, 16*(4-5), 467-471.

[2] Deygers, B., Carlsen, C. H., Saville, N., & Van Gorp, K. (2018). The use of the CEFR in higher education: A brief introduction to this special issue. *Language Assessment Quarterly, 15*(1), 1-2.

（9）Jones, N.

最近著述：

Jones, N., & Ashton, K. (2013). The European survey on language competences. *Academic Exchange Quarterly, 17*(1), 127-132.

（10）Shepard, L.A.

最近著述：

[1] Shepard, L. A., Penuel, W. R., & Pellegrino, J. W. (2018). Using learning and motivation theories to coherently link formative assessment, grading practices, and large-scale assessment. *Educational Measurement: Issues and Practice, 37*(1), 21-34.

[2] Shepard, L. A., Penuel, W. R., & Pellegrino, J. W. (2018). Classroom assessment principles to support learning and avoid the harms of testing. *Educational Measurement: Issues and Practice, 37*(1), 52-57.

（11）Davison, C.

最近著述：

Alonzo, D., Mirriahi, N., & Davison, C. (2019). The standards for academics' standards-based assessment practices. *Assessment & Evaluation in Higher Education, 44*(4), 636-652.

4. 请列出 10 个左右参考文献中出现率高的期刊，去这些期刊的官网浏览最近最新的一期目录，并分享这些期刊的目录截图。

参考作答

tesol international association　　**TESOL QUARTERLY**

CONTENTS

The Curriculum Journal

Volume 31　Number 1　March 2020

Volume 24 Number 2 March 2020

TEACHING
RESEARCH

Language Teaching Research

Contents

EDUCATIONAL MEASUREMENT: ISSUES AND PRACTICE

Volume 38, Number 4
Winter 2019

VOLUME
49

NUMBER
2

CONTENTS

Latest articles

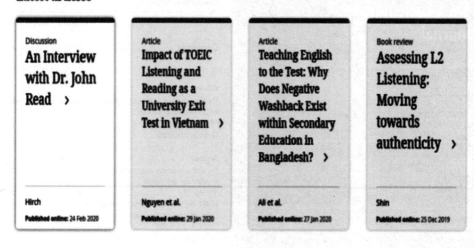

5. 请从 3—4 题的文献中，选出 10 篇左右你感兴趣、与你的专业领域
   或与你的教学和研究密切相关的文献，请浏览其摘要和参考文献，
   谈谈你是否有新的发现。

参考作答 1

Latest articles

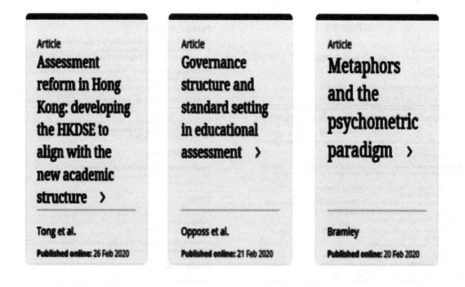

（1）Bartanen, B. (2020). Principal quality and student attendance. *Educational Researcher*, *49*(2), 1-13.

没想到国际权威期刊上的文章也会讨论学生到课率的问题。文章提出一个很新颖的角度，我们以前想提升出勤率都是从教师出发，但作者发现校长的作用也很关键，而且能够提高学生到课率的校长不一定是那些能够提升学生成绩的校长。

（2）Gopalan, M., & Brady, S. T. (2019). College students' sense of belonging: A national perspective. *Educational Researcher*, *49*(2), 134-137.

文章指出在四年制大学中，归属感较强的学生毅力、参与度和心理健康都高于其他学生。这让我想到本次阅读的专著中所强调的学习的社会认知性，对如何促进学习有了新的思考。

（3）O'Dowd, R., Sauro, S., & Spector-Cohen, E. (2019). The role of pedagogical mentoring in virtual exchange. *TESOL Quarterly*, *54*(1), 146-172.

我觉得这篇文献跟我们现在在上网课有关系，看了摘要之后发现，文章主要讲的是跨文化协作，即有不同国家的学习者参与的情况。我粗略看过之后觉得还是很受启发。文章提出了三种网上教学指导方法：1）在上课之前呈现网络互动策略；2）教师指导下的网络互动；3）把学生的网上互动内容融入正式的教学。我们平时上课一般都是采用第二种方法，但根据作者的实验结果，第一种方法可以提高学习共同体的情感和凝聚力，方法三可以促进学生的进一步学习和反思。我觉得对我自己今后的教学有很大的启示作用。

总的来说，没想到从参考文献中可以挖掘出这么多内容，像打开了新世界的大门，也对辜老师一直强调的 Learning by doing 有了深刻的体会，也明白了不是看很多文献就自动能够写出好论文的，批判性思考、问题意识和探究能力都不可或缺。

参考作答 2

浏览了四篇 *Assessment in Education: Principles, Policy and Practice* 上的文献和一篇 *Language Assessment Quarterly* 上的摘要，最大的感触是要跳出自己关注的研究话题，多看看大的测评领域下的研究。浏览的几篇摘要中就涉及测评的宏观层面，比如 government system，以及其他学科，比如 feedback in science。即使在针对英语语言学科的反拨效应研究中，也在讨论 social-psychological, political, economic 等更为复杂的因素。这个研究提到 "A testing-teaching causal relationship may be overly simplistic." 正好呼应在读的著作导读中提到的 "学习并非简单的教与学，学与测，而是一种社会认知行为"。明白自身的局限性，要研究写作测评就不能只关注二语写作领域的测评。

Author Index 补充思考题及参考作答

1. 请思考 Author Index 的目的 / 作用是什么？浏览 Author Index 对你有何意义 / 帮助？

参考作答 1

作用：1）相比较 References 为读者提供专著中引文的出处，Author Index 方便读者查找专著中同一作者的不同引文在什么位置，前者是从专著中的某论点拓展到外部，后者关注的中心就是本专著；2）通过 Author Index 能迅速发现本专著中的高被引学者，进而发现在该领域里值得关注的专家。

意义：以前尚未意识到 Author Index 有何作用，但经过本次的学习，目前明白最重要的意义是我可以通过这个活动真正实践如何查找资料，知道如何根据 Author Index 来开展相关文献的学习和查找。

参考作答 2

这部分是为了方便读者了解书中重要的引用文献的著作者是哪些，分布在书中哪一页，有多少次被书中引用。

结合对参考文献的整理，对引用超过 4 次的作者进行统计之后，可以发现与本书有重要关联的作者有哪些，对进一步了解该领域有重要参考价值。同时，也是一个发现经典著作和经典文献的重要途径，为后续的拓展性阅读指明了方向。

2. 你阅读专著前后是否会看 Author Index？为什么？

参考作答 1

第一次发现 Author Index。

通过这次的阅读，了解了阅读专著前，Author Index 可以帮助读者快速定位本领域的相关学者和机构。在阅读的过程中，应把本部分与参考文献相结合，以加深对专著相关章节所涉及领域的了解。读后可以了解相关的学者和机构，并查阅其研究专长与方向，有哪些代表性著作，进行拓展性阅读，以加深对专著所涉及领域的了解。

参考作答 2

阅读专著前会看 Author Index。

不管是哪本书，都会去看它的每个部分，比如前言、目录、致谢，等等。因为既然它是这本书的一部分，一定有它存在的意义，或多或少能提供一些信息。就像教学生读文本的时候，不能只看正文内容，也要关注图片、标题、字体字号等。以前虽然看了 Author Index，但是没有去思考如何将这些板块的内容为我所用，所以印象不够深刻。这次发现这部分也很有价值。

参考作答 3

第一次知道专著后会有 Author Index，只知道有的会有 Subject index，读专著的时候不太留意 Author Index，但是阅读论文的时候，喜欢阅读参考文献，并通过参考文献寻找更多的文献资料。现在发现其实 Author Index 也很便捷。

3. 请从 Author Index 中选出 10—15 位重现频次高的学者或者你熟悉的学者，查阅他们的著述，尤其是最新、最近的著述，做一份文献目录。请分享你在做这项任务的过程中的收获和遇到的困难。

参考作答

（1）Black, P.

最近著述：

[1] Black, P., & Wiliam, D. (2018). Classroom assessment and pedagogy. *Assessment in Education: Principles, Policy & Practice, 25*(6), 551-575.

[2] Black, P. (2017). Christian beliefs and values in science and religious education: An essay to assist the work of teachers of both subjects. *International Studies in Catholic Education, 9*(2), 206-222.

（2）Broadfoot, P.

最近著述：

[1] Broadfoot, P. (2017). Time to tame the leviathan? Perspectives and possibilities for a new era in assessment. *Assessment in Education: Principles, Policy and Practice, 24*(3), 415-423.

[2] Timmis, S., Broadfoot, P., Sutherland, R., & Oldfield, A. (2016). Rethinking assessment in a digital age: Opportunities, challenges and risks. *British Educational Research Journal, 42*(3), 454-476.

（3）Carless. D.

最近著述：

[1] Carless, D. (2020). Longitudinal perspectives on students' experiences of feedback: A need for teacher-student partnerships. *Higher Education Research and Development, 39*(3), 425-438.

[2] Carless, D. (2015). Exploring learning-oriented assessment processes. *Higher Education, 69*(6), 963-976.

（4）Harlen, W.

最近著述：

Harlen, W. (2013). A rather circular look at effective primary science practices. *Studies in Science Education, 49*(1), 93-98.

（5）Shepard, L.A.

最近著述：

[1] Shepard, L. A., Penuel, W. R., & Pellegrino, J. W. (2018). Using learning and motivation theories to coherently link formative assessment, grading practices, and large-scale assessment. *Educational Measurement: Issues and Practice, 37*(1), 21-34.

[2] Shepard, L. A., Penuel, W. R., & Pellegrino, J. W. (2018). Classroom assessment principles to support learning and avoid the harms of testing. *Educational Measurement: Issues and Practice, 37*(1), 52-57.

（6）Saville, N.

最近著述：

[1] Saville, N. (2019). How can multilingualism be supported through language education in Europe?. *Language Assessment Quarterly, 16*(4-5), 464-471.

[2] Deygers, B., Carlsen, C. H., Saville, N., & Van Gorp, K. (2018). The use of the CEFR in higher education: A brief introduction to this special issue. *Language Assessment Quarterly, 15*(1), 1-2.

（7）Jones, N.

最近著述：

Jones, N., & Ashton, K. (2013). The European Survey on language competences. *Academic Exchange Quarterly, 17*(1), 127-132.

（8）Mislevy, R. J.

最近著述：

[1] Mislevy, R. J. (2019). Advances in measurement and cognition. *The ANNALS of the American Academy of Political and Social Science, 683*(1), 164-182.

[2] Dardick, W. R., & Mislevy, R. J. (2016). Reweighting data in the spirit of

Tukey: Using Bayesian posterior probabilities as Rasch residuals for studying Misfit. *Educational and Psychological Measurement, 76*(1), 88-113.

（9）VanPatten, B.

最近著述：

[1] Lichtman, K., & VanPatten, B. (2021). Was Krashen right? Forty years later. *Foreign Language Annals, 54*(2), 283-305.

[2] Lichtman, K., & VanPatten, B. (2021). Krashen forty years later: Final comments. *Foreign Language Annals, 54*(2), 336-340.

[3] VanPatten, B., & Smith, M. (2018). Word-order typology and the acquisition of case marking: A self-paced reading study in Latin as a second language. *Second Language Research, 35*(3), 1-24.

（10）Davison, C.

最近著述：

Alonzo, D., Mirriahi, N., & Davison, C. (2019). The standards for academics' standards-based assessment practices. *Assessment & Evaluation in Higher Education, 44*(4), 636-652.

遇到的困难：

昨天也有这一题，但是昨天我选择放弃做这个题，原因是我去搜索却没有搜到要求的东西。在昨天整理并阅读了群友的读书笔记之后，运用他们分享的方法去尝试了一下。刚开始的时候发现很困难，后来渐渐找到了一点眉目。所以就找到了以上一些学者的文献。让我感觉特别有收获，渐渐明白老师说的 Learning by doing，也渐渐明白老师给我们列这些思考题的良苦用心，可见分享与同伴学习的重要性。

第一个困难是没有现成的外文数据库可以直接查询。但是可以尝试用群友所共享的资料查询网址去尝试；第二个困难是确定作者名字，发现通过其著作去确定作者是有效的方式。如：Mary James，Institute of Education, University of London, 但其个人学术档案在谷歌学术镜像中相关性不太高，bing 学术可以查到的资料相关性比较高。

4. 请从你做的文献目录中，选出 5—10 篇你感兴趣、与你的专业领域或与你的教学和研究密切相关的文献，请浏览其摘要和参考文献，谈谈这个过程中你是否有新的发现。

参考作答

By filtering among the authors and publications, I found the one whose research was most closely related to LOA.

1) Shepard, L. A. (2018). Learning progressions as tools for assessment and learning. *Applied Measurement in Education, 31*(2), 165-174.

Abstract:

This article addresses the teaching and learning side of the learning progressions literature, calling out for measurement specialists the knowledge most needed when collaborating with subject-matter experts in the development of learning progressions. Learning progressions are one of the strongest instantiations of principles from Knowing What Students Know, requiring that assessments be based on an underlying model of learning. To support student learning, quantitative continua must also be represented substantively, describing in words and with examples what it looks like to improve in an area of learning. For formative purposes, in fact, qualitative insights are more important than scores. By definition, learning progressions require iterative cycles of development so as to build in horizontal coherence among curriculum, instruction, and assessment. Learning progressions are also an important resource for...

Implication：

Learning progression; qualitative insights.

2) Shepard, L. A., Penuel, W. R., & Pellegrino, J. W. (2018). Using learning and motivation theories to coherently link formative assessment, grading practices, and large-scale assessment. *Educational Measurement: Issues and Practice*, 37(1), 21-34.

Abstract:

To support equitable and ambitious teaching practices, classroom assessment design must be grounded in a research-based theory of learning. Compared to other theories, sociocultural theory offers a more powerful, integrative account of how motivational aspects of learning—such as self-regulation, self-efficacy, sense of belonging, and identity—are completely entwined with cognitive development. Instead of centering assessment within systems that support use of interim and end-of-year standardized tests, we argue for a vision of formative assessment based on discipline-specific tasks and questions that can provide qualitative insights about student experience and thinking, including their identification with disciplinary practices. At the same time, to be consistent with a productive formative assessment culture, grading policies should avoid using points and grades "to motivate" students but should create...

Implication：

Sociocultural theory; motivational aspects of learning; grading policies within formative assessment.

3) Shepard, L. A., Penuel, W. R., & Pellegrino, J. W. (2018). Classroom assessment principles to support learning and avoid the harms of testing. *Educational Measurement: Issues and Practice*, 37(1), 52-57.

Abstract:

Shepard, Penuel, & Pellegrino (2018) summarized critically important findings from research on learning and motivation that should be heeded if—as proposed by Mark Wilson (2018) in his Presidential Address to the National Council on Measurement in Education (NCME)—the field of educational measurement were to give greater attention to learning focused classroom assessment. In this short rejoinder we respond to the commentaries provided by Susan Brookhart (2018), Margaret Heritage (2018), Scott Marion (2018), and Dylan Wiliam (2018). There were no major disagreements between ourselves and the four respondents, but this may be because they were selected for their expertise regarding classroom learning as well as large-scale assessment. More broadly, some psychometricians might disagree or might not realize why business-as-usual measurement models should not be applied in classrooms...

Implication:

Learning focused classroom assessment principles.

4) Black, P., & Wiliam, D. (1998). Assessment and classroom learning. *Assessment in Education: Principles, Policy & Practice, 5*(1), 7-74.

Abstract:

This article is a review of the literature on classroom formative assessment. Several studies show firm evidence that innovations designed to strengthen the frequent feedback that students receive about their learning yield substantial learning gains. The perceptions of students and their role in self-assessment are considered alongside analysis of the strategies used by teachers and the formative strategies incorporated in such systemic approaches as mastery learning. There follows a more detailed and theoretical analysis of the nature of feedback, which provides a basis for a discussion of the development of theoretical models for formative assessment and of the prospects for the improvement of practice.

Implication:

Classroom formative assessment, mastery learning.

5) Harlen, W., & James, M. (1997). Assessment and learning: differences and relationships between formative and summative assessment. *Assessment in Education: Principles, Policy & Practice, 4*(3), 365-379.

Abstract:

The central argument of this paper is that the formative and summative purposes of assessment have become confused in practice and that as a consequence assessment fails to have a truly formative role in learning. The importance of this role is argued particularly in relation to learning with understanding (deep learning). It is pointed out that the requirements of assessment for formative and summative purposes differ in several dimensions, including reliability, the reference base of judgements and the focus of the information used. This challenges the assumption that summative judgements can be formed by simple summation of formative ones. An alternative procedure for linking formative and summative assessment is proposed such that their separate functions are preserved.

Implication：

Formative and summative assessment.

6) Shepard, L. A. (2000). The role of assessment in a learning culture. *Educational Researcher*, *29*(7), 4-14.

Abstract:

This article is about classroom assessment—not the kind of assessments used to give grades or to satisfy the accountability demands of an external authority, but rather the kind of assessment that can be used as a part of instruction to support and enhance learning. On this topic, I am especially interested in engaging the very large number of educational researchers who participate, in one way or another, in teacher education. The transformation of assessment practices cannot be accomplished in separate tests and measurement courses, but rather should be a central concern in teaching methods courses.

Implication：

Classroom assessment.

发现：FA 与 SA 的目的很容易混淆（Wiliam & Thompson 1997），用 classroom assessment 则会容易理解些。Classroom assessment 是为了 promote, support and enhance learning（Shepard，2000；Constant Leung et al., 2017），而 feedback 在这个过程中很重要（Black & Wiliam, 1998）。Shepard（2000）指出单独的测试和测量课程并不能完成（教师）测评（素养）训练。因此，为了让以促学为导向的测评实施得更有效，促学测评素养训练应该成为教学法课程的核心，这突出了本书所提倡的 LOA 模式的价值所在，也印证了 LOA 模式是一种教学法的猜想。

Subject Index 思考题及参考作答

1. 请通览 Subject Index，思考它的目的 / 作用，对你有何意义 / 帮助？

参考作答 1

　　和 Author Index 等部分一样，Subject Index 也充当了一个内容地图的作用，将文中出现的术语名词列出，同时附上其出现频率。浏览 Subject Index 有利于更加了解本书的重点和关注内容，并且检验自己是否掌握了相关的知识。例如因为本书主题是 LOA，Subject Index 不仅包含测试常见的 validity，assessment 等术语，而且也包含很多教学相关的内容，如 scaffolding。也列出了一些机构名称，如 Cambridge English，Assessment Reform Group 等，可延伸到机构相关的研究中。

参考作答 2

　　读者基于 Subject Index 能够获取本书主题相关的重要概念术语，出现频率高的概念术语串起来就是专著的中心和主要论述的话题，可以给读者呈现出著作里涉及的所有理论和话题的全貌，其目的是帮助读者快速寻找与主题相关的阅读内容，这是了解书中术语一个重要途径，让读者可以很快找到相关理论在著作中的具体位置。

　　Subject Index 于我的意义是，方便快速地查找感兴趣的话题，正如一篇论文关键词的功能，让读者能在短时间内了解这本书的关键信息。

2. 请勾选出你熟悉的 subjects，并把它们单列出来，看看你会有什么发现？

参考作答 1

　　熟悉的 Subjects：

Accountability	Assessment
Alignment of goals	ARG

Asia	Lifelong
Alternative	Mixed methods
Classroom-based	Monitoring
Dynamic	MOOCS
Formative	Motivation
High-stakes	Natural language acquisition
Summative	New Zealand
Assessment for learning	Policy-makers
Australia	Prior knowledge
Autonomous learner	Private language school
Behaviorist	Professional training
Canada	Qualitative
Can-Do scales	Quantitative
CEFR	Real-world
Classroom activity	Responsibility
Communicative competence	Scaffolding
Curriculum	Second Language Acquisition
Diagnostic assessment	Scotland
Errors	Self-and peer-assessment
Feedback	Teaching to the test
Four worlds of learning	Transfer
Goals	United states
Hong Kong of China	Writing
Learner-centered	Zone of proximal development

发现：1）一边输入这些单词，一边在想如何做名词解释。发现其中自认为很熟悉的 subjects 也不太能把它们解释清楚。有些 subjects 比如 transfer, zone of proximal development, natural language acquisition，需要温故而知新；而有些比如 dynamic assessment，需要更深入了解，不能满足于表面的理解。2）熟悉的 subjects 多偏向于教学实践，而相关理论方面则知之甚少。

参考作答 2

熟悉的 Subjects:

Achievement	Australia
Assessment	Norm-reference
Authentic assessment	Behaviorist
Learner-centred	Curriculum objectives
Big data	Cambridge English
Learning how to learn	Learning objectives
Classroom-based	Canada
Learning interaction	Pass mark
Direct assessment	Can do scales
Learning ladder	Pass rate
Formative assessment	CBA
Lifelong	Performance skills
High-stakes assessment	CEFR
Listening	Policy-makers
Outcomes-based assessment	Classroom activities
Machine learning	PISA
Performance assessment	Communicative competence
MOOCs	PPP
Summative assessment	Computer-based learning interactions
Mixed methods	Pretesting
Sustainable assessment	Constructivism
Motivation	Prior knowledge
Teacher-based assessment	Constructs
Natural language acquisition	Professional training
Assessment for learning	Council of Europe
New Zealand	Qualitative
Assessment literacy	Criterion reference
No Child Left Behind	Quantitative

Critical thinking	Standards
Reading	FA
Curriculum	Task-based approach
Reliability	Goals
Deep and shallow learning	Trait-based
Real-world	Grammaring
Development	Transfer
Scaffolding	Group activities
Dialogue	United States
Schema theory	High-stakes assessment
Diagnostic assessment	Validity
School-based assessment	Hong Kong of China
Errors	Validity and validation
Scotland	impact study
ETS	Washback
SLA	Intended audience
England	Weir's validity framework
Self-and peer-assessment	Intercultural competence
Evidence	Zone of proximal development
Speaking	Writing
Feedback	

发现：熟悉的术语主要有两类，一类是教育学或教育心理学相关的；一类是测试学相关的。

3. 对于不熟悉的 subjects，数一数有多少？这个数字告诉你什么？

参考作答 1

90% 以上都不熟悉。这样的数字告诉我应该要继续加大输入，拓宽自己的视野，不能仅仅局限于自己某一个小的研究方向。

参考作答 2

不熟悉的大约占 60%。这个数字告诉我，科研的路还很漫长，要不断去阅读来拓宽知识面。良好的基础知识储备，是挖掘更深层学术造诣的基础，不能一知半解。

4. 请列出 50 个左右本专著中出现频率高的 subjects，再看看里面有哪些是你熟悉其含义的。对于不熟悉的，请通过各种渠道／资源查阅，并分享你查阅的过程／经历和体会／感悟。

参考作答 1

专著中出现频率高的 subjects:

Achievement	Standards
Qualitative	Dispositions
Classroom assessment	Technology
Quantitative	Evidence
Formative assessment	Transfer
Reading	Feedback
Summative assessment	Validity
Reliability	Goals
Cambridge English	Writing
Responsibility	IRT
Cognition	Group activity
Scaffolding	Learning interaction
CEFR	ESLC
Social constructivism	Listening
Constructs	Ecological
Socio-cognitive model	Meanings
Criterion reference	Emergence
Speaking	Monitoring
Curriculum	English Profile

Motivation	High-order objectives
Action-oriented model	Purposeful usc of languagc
Curriculum objectives	Performance
Construct definition	Qualitative
Learning objectives	Progression
European Commission	Quantitative

体会与感悟：要想办法去解决问题。可以通过互联网的搜索引擎和请教他人来解决术语理解的问题。

参考作答 2

高频 subjects:

Accountability	Feedback
Achievement	Formative
Assessment for Learning	Goals
Assessment Reform Group	Higher-order
Cambridge English	Learning
CEFR	Motivation
Classroom-based	Performance
Cognition	Personal
Construct	Progression
Construct definition	Qualitative
Criterion reference	Reading
Curriculum	Socio-cognitive model
Development	Standards
Direct assessment	Summative
Evidence	Validity
Evidence-centered design	Writing

查阅经历：对于很多高频术语还是比较熟悉的，对于不熟悉的概念，之前买过一本《语言测试词典》，英英对照版很好，但是有时候需要对该名词进行翻译，所以也买了一本中英对照版词典。

第一章 面向学习的测评：概览
Chapter 1　Learning Oriented Assessment: An overview

章节目录

1.思维导图呈现本章目录

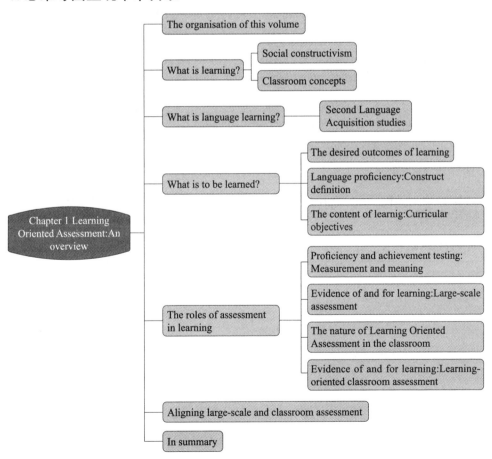

图 1.1　第一章思维导图目录

2. 表格呈现本章目录

表 1.1　第一章表格目录

1 Learning Oriented Assessment: An overview	第一章 面向学习的测评：概览
THE ORGANIZATION OF THIS VOLUME	1.1 本书架构
WHAT IS LEARNING? Social constructivism Classroom concepts	1.2 什么是学习？ 　1.2.1 社会建构主义 　1.2.2 课堂相关的概念
WHAT IS LANGUAGE LEARNING? Second language acquisition studies	1.3 什么是语言学习？ 　二语习得研究
WHAT IS TO BE LEARNED? The desired outcomes of learning Language proficiency: Construct definition The content of learning: Curricular objectives	1.4 学习什么？ 　1.4.1 期待的学习结果 　1.4.2 语言能力：构念定义 　1.4.3 学习内容：课程目标
THE ROLES OF ASSESSMENT IN LEARNING Proficiency and achievement testing: Measurement and meaning Evidence of and for learning: Large-scale assessment The nature of Learning Oriented Assessment in the classroom Evidence of and for learning: Learning-oriented classroom assessment	1.5 测评在学习中的作用 　1.5.1 水平和成就测试：测量及意义 　1.5.2 以评测学和以评促学：大规模测评 　1.5.3 课堂面向学习的测评的本质 　1.5.4 以评测学和以评促学：面向学习的课堂评价
ALIGNING LARGE-SCALE AND CLASSROOM ASSESSMENT	1.6 大规模测评和课堂评价的对接
IN SUMMARY	1.7 小结

补充思考题及参考作答

1. 请结合你的学习、工作或生活经历，谈谈你对作者引用的杜威的话的理解（It requires troublesome work to undertake the alteration of old beliefs.）。

参考作答 1

Our beliefs stem from our personal history, professional history, the context we work and live in, and the aspirations we have for the future. These conditions also apply to the beliefs of educational workers. When new beliefs emerge, especially in the case that the new beliefs contradict with what people usually hold, it could be difficult for people to understand what the new beliefs are about, how to approach them and how to transform them into actual practice. The context in which people work and live may also provide limited conditions for the new beliefs to be realized.

参考作答 2

杜威的这句话是说改变一些旧的观念需要进行一些麻烦的工作。确实，我们的学习工作中处处体现着这一道理。

就拿这次辜老师带我们阅读的活动为例，对我而言就是一次很好的改进以前阅读习惯和阅读方法的机会：如何阅读文献、如何阅读专著、如何在阅读中思考、提出问题以及如何在阅读中答疑。以前自己阅读时没有像现在这样把一本专著的架构了解得这么清楚，现在知道拿到一本专著的读法其实是可以从不同的角度进行的，并不是只从目录和正文开始：我们可以读导读，读本书书评，读不同作者对本书的书评以及本书的中英文书评；在开始读之前就把此书的重点了解了一遍。通过阅读活动还了解到了一些自己以前不曾关注的书中的内容，如 Author Index, Subject Index, List of Tables and Figures; 如何利用 References 扩展阅读。还有，把读过的内容，比如导读，在阅读文章内容时再读，又有不一样的体会。此外，读书不是一个人在读，是大家一起阅读，每个人提出疑问，自己解答，相互解答，老师解答。很多问题已经不再局限于专著本身，思维在阅读和思考中发散。发现阅读、思考、记录的过程看似是 troublesome work，但是对于传统的读书习惯却是一次很好的改进，原来书可以这样读。

教学也是，现在线上网课的教学模式，事实上也是对我们传统的线下教学方式和观念的一种创新，如果不是因为线上教学，我想我们不会这么集中地把这么多课程平台资源和一些录课的 App 的技能在短时间内学到并尽可能使用。

参考作答 3

杜威的话说明要改变原有的理念需要很多繁琐的工作。通过阅读，我发现确实如此。以下是我的反思：

现在这种老师带领大家一起阅读学习是我以前从来没有的经历，如果不是亲身参与我永远体会不到其中的苦辣酸甜，但是更重要的是成长与收获。推及我现在的工作，随着教学发展，教学方式由线下教学转变为线上教学，这个过程中出现过很多问题，到底该如何处理，最初我也很手忙脚乱。但是我们活动开始后，虽然增加了很多阅读的任务和思考，我反而能够更合理地安排时间，很多课余时间都用在了学习上。因为时间有限，考虑更多的是如何解决问题。能够把所学运用于工作实践中，所以我的教学也理顺了。生活中的一些问题也力图做到简化，提高效率。这需要一个过程，需要我们理念的转变与思考，以及行动的付出。这个过程可能出现了，但是我没有意识到，现在老师提出了，就进行有针对性的思考，再次验证老师提问的必要性。

2. 第一章第一段和第二段看上去是否也像是在描述中国外语教学与测评的现状？"We could do better."思考我们作为个体怎样可以做得更好。

参考作答 1

中国外语教学与测评是在不断发展和前进的。《中国英语能力等级量表》

把学生的英语能力进行了一个比较清晰的呈现，从量表的标题就可以看出，能力是首位的，英语语言的应用能力是外语教学的重点。我把《中国英语能力等级量表》的介绍放在这里，以便自己看得清楚些。

《中国英语能力等级量表》（*China's Standards of English*, CSE）以语言运用为导向，将学习者的英语能力从低到高划分为"基础、提高和熟练"三个阶段，共设九个等级，对各等级的能力特征进行了全面、清晰、翔实的描述。能力总表包括语言能力总表，以及听力理解能力、阅读理解能力、口头表达能力、书面表达能力、组构能力、语用能力、口译能力和笔译能力等各项能力总表。

《中国英语能力等级量表》将能力划分为九个等级。其中，一二级大致对应小学水平，三级对应初中，四级对应高中，五六级对应大学，七级对应英语专业，八九级对应高端外语人才。每个等级在听说读写、翻译、知识策略等方面都有不同的要求。

我们作为个体，特别是作为教师，如何在教学中提高学生的语言运用能力，是教学的关键。杜威说的"learning by doing"就强调 doing 的重要性，但如何做是需要我们思考的。我们需要了解一些测评的理论和知识，教学离不开测评，否则学生的学习行为和效果没办法量化。其实平时在教学中我也将形成性评价和终结性评价相结合，但是怎么使评价方式能够对学生的学习能力的提高有帮助，还需要更多思考。

参考作答 2

What the authors describe shares many similarities with the Chinese educational context. For example, the examination orientation, the inefficiency in language teaching and learning, and the conflict between what students should learn, and what should be taught and assessed.

To make things better, it requires efforts from all educational stakeholders, including researchers, teachers, and even school managers. Researchers could conduct more empirical studies regarding classroom teaching and learning so that we know what is actually happening in classrooms and what can be improved. Teachers could open themselves to new ideas, while school managers could create a more stress-free working context for teachers so that they are aware there are no repercussions for them to try new ideas and approaches.

参考作答 3

　　和中国外语教学与测评的现状有些类似。作为一线教师，首先要提高自己的测评素养，清楚学生学习要学什么，测评要测什么。其次，针对学生参加的大规模测试，比如大学英语四六级，英语专业四八级，来设计课堂教学活动和测试，达到大规模测试和课堂评价互补。最后，也要让学生认识到学习的目的不是为了通过每次考试，而是要培养终身学习的习惯和自我学习的能力。

　　作为学习者，思想观念上应该发生改变，学习是为了提升各方面的生活能力，而不是纯粹为了取得更高的分数，因此学习的测评标准不是单一的试卷，而是自己能力的提高和对于所学知识的运用；应该更好地去了解和掌握 Self-assessment，在他评的基础上能够更好地自评，以此不断促进自我学习和提高。最后，我们应该结合现实需求更为高效地学习，在学习的过程中不断观察、评价和反馈。学习和测评应该达到同一个目的，就是提升自我，并且测评应该作为学习的一个促进工具。

3. 如何理解原文作者提到的 "LOA is a vision of radical change and far more effective learning"(p.2 para.3)，其中 radical 具体指什么？以及 radical 表现在哪些方面？

参考作答 1

　　The "radical change" refers to changes in thinking of language assessment. This includes the development of language learning theories and assessment theories, which both drive the development of language assessment. Before LOA or classroom assessment was proposed, assessment was mainly associated with testing. For example, before the 1960s, language testing was primarily informed by the behaviorist theory

(McNamara, 2013). During this period, language testing focused on examining individual language elements, which made discrete point test, such as multiple-choice, true-or-false and spelling tests, a popular choice. Language was considered a bundle of unrelated linguistic elements, not a tool that facilitates communication (Oller, 1979).

Another example is the integrative testing. In the 1970s and 1980s, the communicative approach became influential, and more attention was given to integrative testing, a new approach in language assessment. This strand of thinking considered language competence as a skill that could be performed in the real world and should be assessed with "authentic" tasks that reproduce the language use context (McNamara, 2013). Both discrete point test and integrative testing are widely used as external and internal evaluation tools in educational settings but fail to address what role assessment can play in classroom teaching and learning.

The LOA seeks to combine external testing and classroom assessment to form an ecosystem in which assessment promotes learning and measure and interpret what has been learnt. This would be a radical change compared to LOA's predecessors, which focus mainly on measuring, not learning.

References:

McNamara, T. (2013). Language testing: History, validity, policy. In K. F. Geisinger, B. A. Bracken, J. F. Carlson, J. I. C. Hansen, N. R. Kuncel, S. P. Reise, & M. C. Rodriguez (Eds.), *APA handbook of testing and assessment in psychology* (Vol. 1, pp. 341-352). American Psychological Association.

Oller, J. W. (1979). *Language tests at school: A pragmatic approach*. Longman.

参考作答 2

LOA 是一种从测试主体的角度提出来的观点，是一种测评的范式。关注大规模测评和课堂评价的系统融合。所谓"系统"体现在两个方面，一方面 LOA 使大规模测评和课堂评价互补（complementary/complementarity）（互补之一）

（Figure1.1），另一方面 LOA 把学习的"四个世界"通过任务连接起来（Figure1.2
和 Figure1.3）

LOA 的另一个特征是生态性，即该系统的所有方面和谐共处（互补之二）。
LOA 的系统性和生态性使课堂评价和大规模测评互补促成测评的目的：提供
以评测学（evidence of learning）和以评促学（evidence for learning）（互补
之三）。大规模测评以及课堂评价对测评表现（performance）的解释互补且
存在重合（互补之四）。LOA 的目的就是要明确教师和测评专家之间互补清
晰的职责，为学习提供一个支撑的框架，在课堂教学中这种根本职责属于教
师和学生（互补之五）。

4. Large-scale assessment 描述的 progression 和 classroom assessment 强调的 progress 的区别是什么？

参考作答 1

字典给出的解释 progression: the act of changing to the next stage of development；
progress: movement to an improved or more developed state, or to a forward position。
在大规模测评中，当学生的语言水平从低到高，比如 CEFR 的 A1 到 A2，就
是 progression；在课堂评价中，学生从会说出一个单词到说出两个单词，属于
progress。Progression 更具有信度和效度，通过科学的方式测评而来，也可以用
来描述整个群体水平的变化；progress 相对来说非正式，而更适用于个体，更能
理解书上第 3 页对 Figure 1.1 horizontal dimensions 的解释。

参考作答 2

Progression 更强调大规模测评结果从低到高的一种变化过程以及每一个过程
的共性和特性，而 progress 强调变化过程的体现形式，即使同一个变化过程，表
现形式可能不一样，也就是说处于同一水平的学生其技能水平可能不一样（参照
Figure 1.1）。

5. 在框架介绍方面，作者是按照 2、8、9、3、4、5、6、7 章节的顺序进行编排，这样安排的意图何在？

参考作答 1

This is an odd, but reasonable design. The authors intend to show the readers beforehand where this book will take them so that they (we) will not be lost while reading the summary of the five chapters in the middle. This perhaps corresponds with one of the principles of assessment for learning: remind the learners of their destination of learning. If we know beforehand where the arguments will take us, we might feel less confused while crawling through the reading process.

参考作答 2

在对本书的主体框架做介绍时，作者并没有按照章节的顺序依次介绍，而是先介绍了第 1、2、8、9 章，然后以问题为线索依次介绍其他章节，是否可以理解为他们认为 LOA 在本书中应该最先引起读者的关注，而且这几个章节的介绍也可以让读者在脑海中对书的体系有个整体认识，我们可以清晰地了解本书将阐释 LOA 理论的起因与发展、它的主要理念和构架以及应用。随后几个章节的内容介绍并未按照前面章节介绍的模式，而是通过问题引入，但用了比较大的篇幅介绍其中比较重要的概念和因素，我认为这些章节的内容对 LOA 的理论构建和理解很重要。

6. 如何翻译和理解 "evidence of learning" 和 "evidence for learning" 以及二者分别指什么？二者如何互补?

参考作答 1

For me, the two terms can be interpreted as "以评测学" and "以评促学". Evidence of learning resembles summative assessment which generates evidence of students' achievement in a period. Evidence for learning resembles formative assessment which generates timely evidence of students'performance in class.

参考作答 2

在第 2 页的第 24-25 行找到了两组词的出处。从语法上来看，二者区别在于介词，一个解释为"的"，另一个解释为"为了"，很显然二者表达的意图不一样。从原文的语境来看，LOA 是一种探索课堂评价和大规模测评互补性的方法，兼具系统性和生态性。课堂评价和大规模测试应该共同促成测评的两个重要目的，为学习成果和促进学习提供证据。前者指总结性评价证据，后者指形成性评价证据。

7. 你认为测试的主要目的是什么？我们的语言测试达到预期的目的了吗？

参考作答 1

There are many purposes that assessment could undertake, but I consider the main purpose of assessment should be facilitating students'learning. It is not only classroom assessment's responsibility but also responsibility of large-scale testing. So far, there are rooms for improvement from both perspectives. The importance of classroom assessment should be recognized, and tests should be designed to encourage the building of communicative competence.

参考作答 2

测试的主要目的有两个：筛选和检测。比如高考，一方面可以筛选出优秀的学生，另一方面又检测了他们高中阶段的学习情况。语言测试，比如大学英语四、六级，达到了筛选和检测的目的，分数高的学生确实是平时学习成绩较好、学习能力较强、学习自觉性较高的学生。但是有可能四、六级考察的内容与实际应用还有一些区别，因此才会有人说过了四、六级的人可能不太会用英语以及和英语本族语者交流。即使托福、雅思考出高分的学生，到国外后也要经过一段时间适应才能自如地交流和使用英语。所以，就目前我国语言考试而言，我认为达到了预期目的。

参考作答 3

测试的主要目的应该是为教学服务，可以为教学提供相关证据，促进教学。测试能够了解学生的水平，可以从侧面反映教学效果和学生的学习效果。测试结果虽不是唯一指标，但可以说明问题。

同时，"以评促学"是一个特别好的能激励学生学习的方法，测试还可以设定学习目标，激励学生学习的自觉性。

8. 请谈谈你对大规模测评和课堂评价互补关系的理解。

参考作答 1

Large-scale testing sets up the benchmarks that students should reach, while classroom assessment acts as the enabler on students' way of learning towards the benchmarks.

参考作答 2

大规模测评作为一种更为系统的测试，是经过反复试测和验证的，其结果有一定的说服力，某种程度上能够衡量学生在一段时间内所取得的成就。通过测评结果的比率变化，可以看出整体的教学水平是提高了还是下降了，然后再去分析原因，找出解决方法，反哺课堂教学。但是由于其周期较长，所以不能及时地发现问题并解决问题。而课堂评价作为一种即时性的测验，可以针对学生日常学习进行检测和观察，可以了解每一个阶段学生的学习效果及存在的问题，因此能够很快对教学进行调整。同时能够帮助老师了解学生学习中存在的一些问题，也能够帮助学生自己找到问题，以改进和提高。而课堂评价较为随意，并不如大规模测试那样正式，所以二者形成互补。

9. 本书将回答四个根本性问题：What is learning? What is language learning? What is to be learned? What is the role of assessment in learning? 请谈谈你自己对这四个问题的思考与回答。

参考作答 1

（1）What is learning?

Learning can be the acquisition of new skills, knowledge, and competence. Learning is teaching; when you teach somebody something, you need to learn that something first. Also, learning is doing; doing is learning.

（2）What is language learning?

Language learning is not a one-time thing, but a lifelong pursuit. It goes beyond the conscious awareness of listening, speaking, reading and writing, and even thinking.

（3）What is to be learned?

The appropriate way to think, the way to communicate, the way to live, the way to act, to speak, the right way to see the world.

（4）What is the role of assessment in learning?

For me, appropriate assessment or evaluation may give me a window to see how I (or learners) learn, how much I need to improve, what is wrong with my learning process, and what effort should be given attention to.

参考作答 2

（1）What is learning?

The authors adopt Vygotsky's social constructionism as their learning theory. Building on that, learning is considered a social activity in which students learn through interactions with teachers and more capable peers.

（2）What is language learning and what is to be learned?

I believe these two questions should be considered as one, as our view of language learning will decide what is to be learned in a language classroom. Whether language is a form of knowledge or a tool for communication should be carefully considered, as this will determine the content and constructs taught and assessed in curriculum and assessment. If language is considered a form of knowledge, the curriculum will be designed as a bundle of linguistic knowledge points. If language is considered a tool for communication, the curriculum should be designed to promote active engagement with authentic materials and to encourage active use of language.

（3）What is the role of assessment in learning?

Assessment can be used for both summative and formative purposes, measuring achievement and facilitating learning. But the ultimate goal should be promoting learning, no matter what forms of assessment have been adopted. Evidence of students' learning progress can be extracted from both forms of assessment. Both sources can contribute to teachers' decision of instructions that will help students improve.

10. 请谈谈你如何理解作者定义的 LOA。

参考作答 1

LOA is an assessment system that includes both the use of large-scale testing and classroom assessment. Large-scale testing reflects the learning objectives and content that a specific language level requires and provide the summative records reporting on students' performances, while classroom assessment facilitates classroom teaching and learning, allowing teachers to make proper instructions to students so that they can move forward to meet the language level requirement specified in large-scale testing.

参考作答 2

LOA 从考试主体的视角出发，利用大规模测评和课堂评价的合力，把四个世界有机结合起来，以获取更全面的证据，实现更好的教育测量和更佳学习效果的双重目标，最终培养学生的学习品格、态度和能力，使之能够超越专业知识、融汇学科技能、持续学习、终身学习和全面发展（李亮，2018）。

11. 社会建构主义理论是如何作用并影响 LOA 的？

参考作答

建构主义强调学习者的主动性，认为学习是学习者基于原有的知识和经验生成意义、建构理解的过程，而这一过程常常是在社会文化互动中完成的。从建构主义角度而言，如果能够将课程、教学、测评和社会融合在一起去促进学习，那么教育的目的性和连贯性就可以得到保障，课程学习目标的达成和学习者终身学习能力的养成就有实现的可能，而《欧框》的研制就是这种可能的一个范例。基于《欧框》，LOA 致力于培养学生的学习能力，促进其终身学习，力图为教育状况的改变提供新的思路。

建构主义对教学和学习具有重要的意义，而社会建构主义则进一步强调学习的社会性和合作性。建构主义，尤其是社会建构主义，让人们深思"学习"的本质，而"二语习得"作为"学习"的一种特例，也需要探讨学习的社会属性，这也促进了 LOA 的研究。

12. "四个世界"以"任务"为中心联系并交互作用，为什么是以"任务"为中心，而不是以"目标"为中心，在语言测试学里还有其他方面的解释吗？

参考作答 1

在社会工作专业领域，"任务中心模式"是个案工作的一种社会工作模式，可追溯到 20 世纪 60 年代，为了回应当时在个案工作开展过程中服务效率低下的实际问题，雷依德（William J. Rei）和沙尼（Annw Shyne）合作开展了一项为了促进个案工作服务效率的研究。1972 年，雷依德和艾泼斯坦（Laura Epstein）合作出版了《任务中心个案工作》一书，具体讲述在有限的时间内实现由服务对象自己选定明确目标的任务中心模式。在任务中心模式看来，任务就是服务对象为解决自己的问题而需要做的工作。它是服务介入工作的核心，是实现服务介入工作目标——解决问题的手段。两者之间的关系类似于目标和手段之间的联系。解决问题是目标，任务是实现解决问题的手段。

从社会工作实践的角度来看，在运用任务实现目标过程中非常关注服务对象的自主性，一方面服务对象具有处理自己问题的权利和义务，即由服务对象自己决定是否需要处理问题、处理什么问题以及怎样处理问题等，提高服务对象的参与程度；另一方面，服务对象具有解决自己问题的潜在能力，即社会工作者在服务介入过程中尽可能发挥服务对象自身拥有的潜在能力，提高服务对象解决问题的能力。

我依据本书给出的答案在 p.5 以及 p.6 第一完整自然段，原因有三个：1）因为 tasks 与这"四个世界"的每个世界都有联系；2）突显进行有意义交流的学习者的认知发展的重要性，以及利用 tasks 围绕具有社会价值的共同目标来连接不同世界的实际用途；3）tasks 通过自然习得和正规教学实现学习。

参考作答 2

任何教学目标和测评目标都要最终以具体"任务"的形式呈现出来，"目标"是相对共性的、抽象的，没有办法执行，需要分解成多个"任务"具体实施；而"任务"是比较具体的、可达成的，所以在真正的学习中，"任务"促使学习发生。

13. LOA 模式的生态性体现在哪里？

参考作答 1

根据书中和之前导读中的解释，LOA 的生态性主要在于强调形成性评价和终结性评价并非两个对立的概念和操作，它们之间是互补关系，是共存共生的，并且服务于一个共同的目标，即促进学习，让可持续性学习成为每个受教育者的一种能力。

参考作答 2

LOA 模式构建了"四个世界"，并将四者以"任务"为驱动形成环状，以服务于"学习"的目的。这四个世界分别指"个人""教育""社会""测评"。"个人"运用"任务"发展个体的认知；"教育"运用"任务"设计课堂练习、组织正式教学；"社会"运用"任务"评价技能表现；"测评"以"任务"为测量基础。通过"任务"驱动实现了两种方式的"学习"：在现实世界中通过参与"任务"实现自然习得和在正式教育环境中通过接受教育实现学习。通过四个世界，个人、教育、社会、测评构成了一个连贯的有机体，体现了 LOA 模式的生态性。

14. 请解读本章中的 5 张图，每一张图的呈现有什么不理解或不清楚的，或文中没有解释充分甚至缺失的地方。

参考作答 1

I would like to challenge Figure 1.2 and 1.3. From my perspective, the world of assessment should not be displayed as an independent section in the "four worlds". As the authors argue, the world of assessment links other worlds together. The world of assessment exists within the arrows that connect the other three worlds. It is more like a thread that weaves the three worlds together, not an independent section of the system. The learning section in Figure 1.3 also seems misplaced to me. From my perspective, the learning section should be integrated with the assessment section, as learning and assessment should be the two sides of a coin. The four ingredients of the learning section, i.e., tasks, interaction, observation, and feedback, are also key features of formative assessment, which cannot be separated from the LOA system. The two figures might be better designed if changed to a triangular model, with assessment and learning placed at the center.

参考作答 2

"Figure1.1 A Complementary relationship between large scale and classroom assessment" (p.3) illustrates that either one has its own merits, and they have the complementary roles in LOA.

"Figure1.2 Four worlds of learning" (p.4) shows that learning connects the four worlds, that is, the personal world, the social world, education, and assessment, and the last one brings together the other three worlds. My question is why there isn't a reverse arrow from the social world to assessment or whether it is blocked by the head of the figure.

"Figure1.3 The four worlds linked by a focus on task" (p.5) shows the central position of tasks which link the worlds through a learning cycle based on the performance of a task, observation, and feedback. Tasks are placed at the center because they have relevance to each of the four worlds. My question is why interaction is placed here without any explanation.

第二章 面向学习的测评源起
Chapter 2 The roots of Learning Oriented Assessment

章节目录

1. 思维导图呈现本章目录

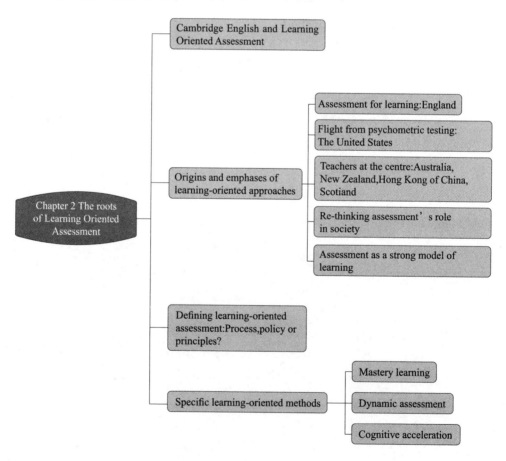

图 2.1 第二章思维导图目录

2. 表格呈现本章目录

表2.1　第二章表格目录

2 The roots of Learning Oriented Assessment	第二章 面向学习测评的源起
CAMBRIDGE ENGLISH AND LEARNING ORIENTED ASSESSMENT	2.1 剑桥英语和面向学习的测评
ORIGINS AND EMPHASES OF LEARNING-ORIENTED APPROACHES Assessment for learning: England Flight from psychometric testing: The United States Teachers at the centre: Australia, New Zealand, Hong Kong of China, Scotland Re-thinking assessment's role in society Assessment as a strong model of learning	2.2 面向学习的方法源起和重点 2.2.1 以评促学：英国 2.2.2 心理测量学的飞跃：美国 2.2.3 以教师为中心：澳大利亚、新西兰、中国香港、苏格兰 2.2.4 重新思考测评在社会中的作用 2.2.5 测评——一个强大的学习模式
DEFINING LEARNING-ORIENTED ASSESSMENT: PROCESS, POLICY OR PRINCIPLES?	2.3 面向学习的测评定义：过程、政策或原则？
SPECIFIC LEARNING-ORIENTED METHODS Mastery learning Dynamic assessment Cognitive acceleration	2.4 特定的面向学习的方法 2.4.1 掌握学习 2.4.2 动态测评 2.4.3 认知加速

补充思考题及参考作答

1. 第二章作者为什么引用杜威这句话（The value of any fact or theory as bearing on human activity is, in the long run, determined by practical application—that is by using it for accomplishing some definite purpose.)? 换言之，引用杜威这句话与本章内容有何关联？

参考作答 1

　　这句话可以作为教学过程中使用 task 的理论依据。使用 task 的目的就是让学习者能够通过实践的方式来运用所学，检测所学效果，进而制定下一步的学习计划。以社会建构主义为理论依据的面向学习的测评，目的就是建立一个以 task 为中心的生态学习系统，让学习者在完成 task 的同时达到高层次的目标，即交际技巧。所以，杜威的这句话点出了面向学习的测评的核心，就是要通过实际运用所学达成一定的目的。

参考作答 2

本章讲 LOA 源起与发展，作者在这里引用这句话，主要是想说任何理论的价值都是以人类活动为基础，如果失去了人类活动这个载体，任何理论和事实都会失去意义。一个理论能否长久发展取决于实际运用，作者在本章提出了 LOA 源起与发展，也正是呼应了这句话。我们需要一些更好的测评方法，所以产生了 LOA。正是因为我们在学习与测评的过程中不断地运用它，它才能够长久发展到现在。

参考作答 3

第二章的主要内容是追溯 LOA 的源起，介绍 LOA 的背景、定义及使用方法等。此处引用杜威的话应该是为了表示 LOA 的源起和发展首先是出于现实考虑，同时要实际运用这个理论，落到实处才能使其更好地发展，作者希望一线教师能够真正将 LOA 理论运用于教学实践，实现促进学习的目的。当然，这是一个漫长的过程。吾将上下而求索。

2. 请问"面向学习的测评"在中国环境下的现状如何？

参考作答

Carless (2007), reporting on a project in Hong Kong of China, claims to be the first to use the term Learning Oriented Assessment. As he explains, he coined the term in an attempt to emphasize the learning features of assessment and promote their development, but also to distance it from the term "formative" through its various forms of interpretation in Hong Kong of China which had acquired negative connotations among teachers.

3. 你赞同测评是一种学习模式吗？为什么？

参考作答 1

I would agree, under the condition that the inferences of assessment have been drawn and used in a way that facilitates learning. If the results of the assessment have been analyzed to provide evidence that guides teaching and learning, then the assessment is a part of the learning process. However, if the results have not been used to inform future teaching and learning, it is not used as a part of learning.

参考作答 2

赞同，学习是社会交流的产物（p.54），通过学习，人们可以提升自我认知水平和加深对外部世界的认知。在学习过程中以任务为依托，通过观察、实践、反馈的循环不断修正并逐渐形成对事物的正确认知。在这个过程中，测评可以为"修正"提供依据和参照，让学习者明确自己所处的位置与目标之间的距离，从而主动调整下一步的学习方法，以此达到理想的学习目标；并且测评过程本身也是修正和自我完善的过程。因此，测评既是学习过程不可或缺的一部分，也是一种学习模式。

参考作答 3

赞同。测评和其他的学习模式有很多共同之处。测评之前，可以使用"以评促学"的方法，参加测评前会主动进行相关内容的搜索式学习，学习新知、温习旧知，不断地提升和改进；测评过程中以及测评后反馈的结果能更清晰地了解学习过程中的不足，采取一定的措施不断地进行修正和调整。在一线教学中，随着课标的不断更新和修改，越来越强调教—学—评一体化，测评、教学和学习密不可分，因此测评也是一种学习模式。

4. 请问面向学习的三种方法，你倾向于使用哪一种？为什么？

参考作答 1

The cognitive acceleration is more favorable to me, as it is in line with Vygotsky and Piaget's conception of what learning should be like. The book provides descriptions of how each stage in cognitive acceleration should be like, which makes the technique sound more doable. However, I would like to find a case that brings this technique into use in a real-life classroom context so that I can be truly persuaded that it is manageable for teachers.

参考作答 2

我更倾向于 mastery learning，定期对自我的学习进行测评和反馈能够帮助我更好地了解自己的学习情况，也能够对下一阶段的学习做好规划。我认为学习是一个比较连续的阶段，如果前面部分有很多问题没有搞懂，而自己也没有找出问题在哪里的话，很难更好地进行下一阶段的学习。

参考作答 3

我更倾向于 Mastery learning。本科阶段学习《语言学概论》这门课时，我参考了不同版本、利用了不同资源来学习，直至把一个个抽象的概念弄懂。这样不仅能够加深自己对概念的理解，也能让自己从不同的角度去思考同一个问题，反思自己在教育见习、实习中遇到的问题。在教学时，我们可能会抱怨教材的种种不合理性，遇到自己比较了解的话题，可能会多向学生介绍，但遇到自己不熟悉或者不了解的话题，就会介绍得少一些。这样下来，学生对于不熟悉话题的学习可能就不会那么深入。解决此类问题，我觉得我们还是可以从教材本身出发，找到不同版本、不同体裁的阅读文本，鼓励学生加强输入，直至他们能够内化。

5. 请用第二章中列出的一些面向学习的测评 / 以评促学的 principles, factors, aspects（pp.24, 28, 29, 30, 139–141, 142–143）对自己的教或学和我们的读书活动做自评。

参考作答 1

　　We can interpret our literature-reading tutoring activity from the perspectives of both social constructivism and social cognitive theory. From social constructivism perspective: the new situation or new problem the members (as a learning community) were involved in or ran into was to grasp the theory and practice of LOA. During the process, the members within themselves and the members and the tutor needed to cooperate and dialogue with each other. In addition, the tutor gave mediation and guidance upon the members' learning. At last, the members were expected to internalize and construct their framework of knowledge and tactics of LOA. From the perspective of social cognitive theory: during the process of literature-reading tutoring, the novice teachers tended to observe and imitate tutor's or peer's practice, which enabled them to acquire the new information of LOA more quickly. Their whole acquisition process was expected to experience four stages, e.g., attentional processes, retention processes, production processes and motivational processes.

参考作答 2

　　For me, every question raised by Prof. Gu and other colleagues in the reading group is an assessment task that drives me to re-think about the reading I have done. These tasks stimulate my learning, motivate me to engage in discussion, and have obviously done the same thing to many other colleagues in the group. The feedback from Prof. Gu and other colleagues have also supported my thinking and showed me new perspectives of understanding the book.

参考作答 3

Assessment should involve students actively in engaging with criteria, quality, their own and/or peer performance (P.24).

读书活动在 our own/peer performance 方面做得很充分，是通过第三点中提到的 timely feedback 实现的。辜老师每天及时整理所有读者的作业并进行反馈，这样让我很有动力每天去查阅读者作业点评，这个过程中可以看到别人的想法并与自己的进行对比，我觉得是一种 assessment as learning，很受启发。我在想这个模式可不可以用于日常写作教学，在写作教学中进行同伴互评。很多时候我们会认为互评应是让学生互相之间改错误，其实互相展示同学的作文，就像我们现在看其他读者的作业一样，可能也会激励同学们进行自我评价。当同学们看到老师给其他同学的评价，也会去做这些 scaffolding（教师反馈＋同伴作文）信息下的自我评价。

要认识到评价对学生动机和自尊的影响（P.28）。

我觉得我对于 motivation 一词的理解还很不够，会觉得鼓励式教育就可以保护学生的学习动力，但是长期的鼓励好像也会使学生缺乏动力。第四点关于学生的自我评价，对我自己来说，现在对自己做出客观的自我评价真的挺难。就像现在每天完成作业之后，我其实对自己的作业质量都不太满意。我突然想到了小时候别人会问"考试考得怎么样啊"，我的回答一定是"不知道"，因为自己不敢评价，怕最后的结果和现在的回答矛盾。这个心理到现在都很影响我做事的信心，但是当我有了外部支持，一定会做得更好。

参考作答 4

One principle of assessment for learning (Assessment Reform Group 2002): Assessment for learning should be part of effective planning of teaching and learning.

以评促学应当是有效教学的一部分。学习者如何获得反馈，他们如何参与自评及他们如何获得发展都应当在计划之列。回顾曾经的高中教学经历，我曾做过这样的尝试：为了帮助高三的学生短期快速积累，我找出三十多篇优秀的短文（其中包括优秀作文），提前告知学生测评的目的和方式，要求他们每周记忆两篇文章，先抽查朗读背诵，再默写。我会及时检查他们的进度，并给出反馈。背诵的目的是通过反复朗读，重复记忆，提升词句的语感。默写是为了加深词汇的印象，增加词句的储备量。刚开始学生很吃力，但为了提升，他们都能坚持下来。当他们写作遇到难以表达的句子时，可以借鉴曾经背诵过的句子，加以模仿。通过四届高三的教学尝试，我感觉这样的方式的确帮助学生在作文方面提升不少。

6. 你是如何判断每章中引用的文献哪些是代表性的或重要的文献？请列举本章引用的 3—5 篇代表性的文献。请查阅我国的关于面向学习的测评的代表性文献，并按《外语教学与研究》的文献规范进行整理。

参考作答 1

（1）Important literature is usually frequently cited in the book and other pertinent literature. To judge whether an article or a book is representative, we need to be familiar with not only this book but also other related literature. I consider the following literature cited in this chapter important and representative:

Assessment Reform Group. (2002). *Assessment for learning*: 10 *principles*. University of Cambridge.

Black, P., & Wiliam, D. (1998). Assessment and classroom learning. *Assessment in Education: Principles, Policy & Practice, 5*(1), 7-74.

Black, P., & Wiliam, D. (2009). Developing the theory of formative assessment. *Educational Assessment, Evaluation and Accountability, 21*(1), 5-31.

Davison, C., & Leung, C. (2009). Current issues in English language teacher-based assessment. *TESOL Quarterly, 43*(3), 393-415.

Mansell, W., James, M., & Assessment Reform Group. (2009). Assessment in schools: Fit for purpose? A commentary by the teaching and learning research program. London: Economic and Social Research Council, Teaching and Learning Research Program.

（2）Some of the Chinese literature regarding learning-oriented assessment:

郭茜，杨志强．试论形成性评价及其对大学英语教学与测试的启示 [J]. 清华大学教育研究，2003，24(5)：103-108.

金艳．体验式大学英语教学的多元评价 [J]. 中国外语，2010，7(1)：68-111.

赵德成．教学中的形成性评价：是什么及如何推进 [J]. 教育科学研究，2013，(3)：47-51.

参考作答 2

（1）一般会根据引用的内容做初步的判断，如提到 the first to... 之类的会觉得应该很权威；看这个引用作者名字是否熟悉、看发表的时间；翻参考文献，看完整的题目以及发表期刊。

Black, P., & Wiliam, D. (1998). Assessment and classroom learning. *Assessment in Education: Principles, Policy & Practice*, 5(1), 7-73.

Carless, D. (2007). Learning-oriented assessment: Conceptual bases and practical implications. *Innovations in Education and Teaching International*, 44(1), 57-66.

Mansell, W. (2010). *The Assessment Reform Group: 21 years of investigation, argument and influence*. Cambridge Assessment Network.

（2）使用"面向学习的测评"这个关键词，在知网上没有搜索到相关文献，但是搜索到一篇关于形成性评价的文章。

赵德成．教学中的形成性评价：是什么及如何推进 [J]. 教育科学研究，2013，(3)：47-51.

第三章　什么是学习?
Chapter 3　What is learning ?

章节目录

1. 思维导图呈现本章目录

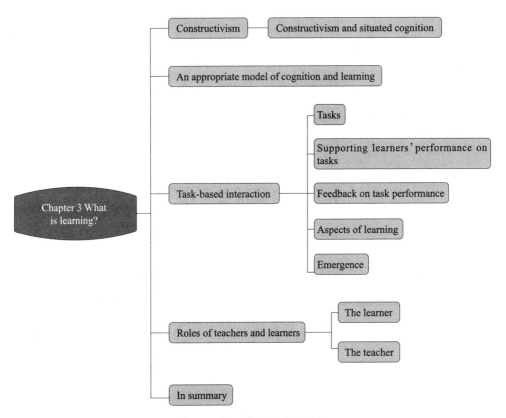

图 3.1　第三章思维导图目录

2. 表格呈现本章目录

表 3.1　第三章表格目录

3 What is learning?	第三章 什么是学习?
CONSTRUCTIVISM Constructivism and situated cognition	3.1 建构主义 　3.1.1 建构主义与情景认知
AN APPROPRIATE MODEL OF COGNITION AND LEARNING	3.2 一个适合的认知和学习模型
TASK-BASED INTERACTION Tasks Supporting learners' performance on tasks Feedback on task performance Aspects of learning Emergence	3.3 任务型互动 　3.3.1 任务 　3.3.2 支持学习者的任务表现 　3.3.3 任务表现反馈 　3.3.4 学习的方方面面 　3.3.5 涌现
ROLE OF TEACHERS AND LEARNERS The learner The teacher	3.4 教师和学习者的角色 　3.4.1 学习者 　3.4.2 教师
IN SUMMARY	3.5 小结

补充思考题及参考作答

1. 你是否赞同杜威的教育观（Education is a social process; education is growth; education is not preparation for life but is life itself.）？为什么？或用杜威的教育观来审视自己的教育观与教育实践，有何异同？

参考作答 1

　　赞同。

　　教育是一种社会进程，教育就是成长，教育不是为生活而做准备，它就是生活本身。个体进入社会，是通过教育活动来获取社会属性的。教育可以使得个体在知识、技能等各方面得以成长。

第一，教育包括家庭教育、学校教育和社会教育，其中最重要的是家庭教育。身处教师行列的我们，在教育别人孩子的同时，也别忽视了自己孩子的教育。自己孩子的教育经历正好为自身教学内化理论提供实践检验。

第二，教师在教育过程中，也是在不断学习成长的。通过学习、思考、反馈和提升，来实现教师从"新手"到"老手"的过渡。从这些年的教育教学来看，在理论充电过程中，我不仅收获了新知识，更多的是提升了教育教学思维的高度，获取更多的视角来帮助解决实际问题。

第三，就学习者本身，他们在建构自身的知识体系、认知发展和养成学习品格的过程，就是一种成长。

参考作答 2

赞同杜威的教育观。

因为教育就是一个社会过程，就像有人曾经说过"No person is an island!"，每一个个体都是社会的一部分，那么个体所从事的活动就是社会进程的一部分。教育就是一种成长，无论是获取知识和培养能力，还是在此过程中与老师和同伴的交流，甚至是自我学习（与书籍作者的交流），以及发现问题并解决问题，这都是一种成长。教育不是为生活做准备，因为教育本身就是生活。正如我刚刚说到的，教育是一种个体活动，任何活动都是生活的一部分，尽管我们有时候可能没有意识到，但是这种活动本身就是生活的一种体现形式。

以前，我认为教育就是一种有意识的、有意义的教学行为，而且教育提供的内容要么是一种明晰的知识，要么是非常确切的定论或者结论。但是今天看到辜老师的点评，忽然有所感触，这和我今天看到的孙立平教授（清华大学社会学系教授、博士生导师）的观点不谋而合，思考也是教育（比知识更高层次的教育）。正如著名的教育家叶圣陶先生所说：教学有法，教无定法，贵在得法。我现在理解所谓的"法"，就是教育的实质，教育是一种方式和手段，其本质是生活。没有人规定，什么样才是好的生活，各有各的活法，但是好的活法就是既要生存，又要成长和进步，这就是教育。

参考作答 3

赞同杜威的教育观。

"Education is not a matter of indoctrination, it is a lighting of fire." 杜威的教育观认为教育即成长和生活，将教育融合在生活中，在生活实践中进行学习，也就是将学习变成一个 life-long 的过程，不断学习，不断成长。

这个教育可以是来自学校的正式教育，可以是来自生活实践中的教育，也可以是来自老师、同伴或者身边其他人的教育；同时也可以创建和加入学习社区，跟不同群体的伙伴一起交流、共同进步，这种社会化的学习过程跟杜威的主张是相似的。反观自身的教育观，把对学生的教育狭隘化，只是仅限于课堂上的教育，对于其他的关注较少。

2. 请抄写或打印一遍本章的详细目录，包括每节中的 sub-headings，谈谈你在梳理过程中的新理解和新发现。

参考作答 1

（1）本章目录：

Chapter 3 What is learning?

3.1 Constructivism

3.1.1 Constructivism and situated cognition

3.2 An appropriate model of cognition and learning

3.3 Task-based interaction

3.3.1 Tasks

3.3.2 Supporting learners' performance on tasks

　　Explicit criteria

　　Scaffolding

　　Goals

3.3.3 Feedback on task performance

3.3.4 Aspects of learning

3.3.5 Emergence

3.4 Roles of teachers and learners

3.4.1 The learner

　　Self- and peer-assessment

　　Motivation

3.4.2 The teacher

　　The teacher's role in learning

　　The teacher's role in classroom assessment

　　The teacher's role in summative assessment

3.5 In Summary

（2）发现：

整理过程中，对本章的框架有了更清楚的认识。本章首先介绍了 LOA 的理论基础——建构主义。其次介绍了 LOA 实施的环境——以任务为基础的课堂互动。在这样的课堂互动中，老师和学生共同建构学习。老师的角色是支持学生的表现，具体可以在完成任务过程中给出清晰的标准、提供支架、学生共同设立目标。在任务完成后可以给出好的反馈，而好的反馈应当是促进学习的。当学习者在老师的支持下通过互动完成课堂任务时，学习者能够有目的地使用语言交流，就从表面学习上升到了深度学习。就教师和学习者的角色而言，在面向学习的课堂中，学习的责任就由老师转向了学习者。因此，教师要学习更专业的测评知识，提高测评素养。

梳理完之后，我开始反思我的课堂教学，如何达到师生共同构建？如何扮演好教师的角色？如何帮助学生扮演好学习者的角色？认识到自己还有很多的知识需要学习。

参考作答 2

发现：

在梳理过程中对这一章的框架更加了解，作者在 3.1 先介绍了建构主义以及 LOA 中对 learning 的定义是基于建构主义的，3.2 介绍了 LOA model 的形成过程，

3.3 和 3.4 则介绍了 learning-oriented classroom interactions 的组成部分：tasks，scaffolding，feedback，roles of students and teachers 以及与其相关的内容，3.5 则是对整个 chapter 的一个总结，但是对于 3.2 An appropriate model of cognition and learning 及其内容的安排并不是非常明确。

参考作答 3

发现：整理完之后我认为本章作者围绕 What is learning? 从三个方面展开。3.1 与 3.2 是理论基础介绍；3.3 作为主体部分阐述 LOA 的学习是 Task-based interaction；3.4 是关于在 Task-based interaction 学习中教师和学生的角色。这个写作思路是从理论逐渐聚焦到教育实践主体上。

疑惑：1）3.1 部分没有 3.1.2，并且我觉得从标题上很难反映出 social constructivism 对 LOA 的重要性；2）3.3.5 Emergence 为什么要单列小标题，虽然这个概念更强调从有意识的学习到高阶能力的实质变化，但它不属于 3.3.4 aspects of learning 吗？

参考作答 4

发现：

整理之后，基于本章的各级标题，对本章重要的内容有了更清晰的了解，例如：对 Task-based interaction 包含的重要因素如 tasks，prior knowledge，explicit criteria，scaffolding，goals 重新进行了回顾。本章拓展了我对学习理解的广度和深度，让我重新审视自己的教学设计框架。

但是也发现作者在进行 3.4 Roles of teachers and learners 写作时，并未统一格式，例如先写了学习者而非教师；虽然对于教师在学习、课堂评价和终结性测试中的作用从标题中看起来进行了区分解释，但 3.4.1 The learner 小标题的位置排列有点让人不理解。

3. 请按照本章中文献出现的先后顺序做一份本章的 References，重复的文献按顺序重复排列。请谈谈你在梳理过程中是否有新理解和新发现。

参考作答

（1）本章的参考文献：

Jonassen, D., & Land, S. (2012). *Theoretical foundations of learning environments*. Routledge.

Sjøberg, S. (2007). Constructivism and learning, In in E. Backer, B. McGaw, & P. Peterson (Eds.) , *International encyclopedia of education* (3rd edition, pp.485-490). Elsevier.

Sjøberg, S. (2007). Constructivism and learning, In in E. Backer, B. McGaw, & P. Peterson (Eds.), *International encyclopedia of education* (3rd edition, pp.485-490). Elsevier.

Vygosky, L. (1986). *Thought and language*. MIT Press.

Vygosky, L. (1978). *Mind in society*. Harvard University Press.

Black, P., & William, D. (2009). Developing the theory of formative assessment. *Educational Assessment, Evaluation, and Accountability*, *21*(1), 5-31.

Wilson, D., & Black, P. J. (1996). Meanings and consequences: A basis for distinguishing formative and summative functions of assessment? *British Educational Research Journal*, *22*(5), 537-554.

Wilson, D., & Black, P. J. (1996). Meanings and consequences: A basis for distinguishing formative and summative functions of assessment? *British Educational Research Journal*, *22*(5), 537-554.

Saville, N. (2009). Developing a model for investigating the impact of language assessment with educational context by a public examination provider, unpublished thesis, University of Bedfordshire.

Frederiksen, N., Mislevy, R. J. & Bejar, I. (Eds). (1993). *Test theory for a new generation of tests.* Lawrence Erlbaum Associates.

Misley, R. J., Steinberg, L. S., & Almond, R. G. (1998). *Evidence-centered assessment design.* Educational Testing Service.

Xu, X., & von Davier, M. (2006). Cognitive diagnosis for NAEP proficiency data, available online: onlinelibrary.

Pellegrino, J. W., Chudowsky, N., & Glaser, R. (2001). *Knowing what students know: The science and design of educational assessment.* National Academy Press.

Shepard, L. A. (2000). The role of assessment in a learning culture. *Educational Researcher, 29* (7), 171-183.

James, M., & Brown, S. (2005). Grasping the nettle: Preliminary analysis and some enduring issues surrounding the improvement of learning outcomes. *The Curriculum Journal, 16*(1), 7-30.

Pellegrino, J. W., Chudowsky, N., & Glaser, R. (2001). *Knowing what students know: The science and design of educational assessment.* National Academy Press.

Teasdale, A., & Leung, C. (2000). Teacher assessment and psychometric theory: A case of paradigm crossing? *Language Testing, 17*(20), 163-184.

Jones, N. (2012). Reliability and dependability, In G. Fulcher & F. Davidson, (Eds.) *The Routledge handbook of language testing* (pp. 364-376). Routledge.

Sayer, A. (1992). *Method in social science: A realistic approach.* Hutchinson.

Shavelson, R. J. (2008). Guest editor's introduction. *Applied Measurement in Education, 21*(4), 293-294.

Shavelson, R. J. (2009). Reflections on learning progressions, paper presented at the Learning Progression in Science (LeaPS) Conference.

（2）发现：

首先，这一章引用很多，理论支撑很强，LOA 是一个综合性较强的模型。从现在梳理的文献来看，文献来源很广，涉及教育学、测试等领域的专著、期刊论文和会议论文，启示我们要广泛搜索和阅读文献。其次，多次引用的文献，可以作为拓展阅读的书目。最后，发现了一个期刊，*Educational Assessment,*

Evaluation, and Accountability，接下来会重点关注。

4. 请梳理和列出本章中的重要概念。对每一个概念请抄一遍专业的解释，并注明出处。请谈谈你在此过程中对这些概念是否有新理解和新发现。

参考作答

Cognitive/social constructivism: Two key features of cognitive constructivist views of learning are that learners construct their own understanding by developing mental models and that existing knowledge has an important role in this development. In socio-cultural constructivist perspectives on learning there is also a focus on understanding but through "making sense of new experience with others" rather than by working individually. (Harlen, 2013, p. 32)

Zone of proximal development (ZPD): ZPD is the distance between the actual developmental level as determined by independent problem solving and the level of potential development as determined through problem solving under adult guidance or in collaboration with more capable peers. (Vygotsky, 1978, p. 33)

Scaffolding: Scaffolding is a process that enables a child or novice to solve a task or achieve a goal that would be beyond his unassisted efforts. (Wood, Bruner, & Ross, 1976, p. 90)

Feedback: Feedback is information about the gap between the actual level and the reference level of a system parameter which is used to alter the gap in some way. (Ramaprasad, 1983, p. 4)

References

Harlen, W. (2013). A rather circular look at effective primary science practices. *Studies in Science Education*, *49*(1), 93-98.

Vygotsky, L. (1978). *Mind in society.* Harvard University Press.

Wood,D., Bruner, J. S., & Ross, G. (1976). The role of tutoring in problem solving. *Journal of Child Psychology and Psychiatry, 17*(2), 89-100.

Ramaprasad, A. (1983). On the definition of feedback. *Behavioral Science, 28,* 4-13.

5. 请梳理和列出本章中提到的理论。对每一个理论请查阅至少一篇综述文章，阅读并附上文献的摘要。请列一份文献目录，并分享你的目录和查到的文献（以 PDF 文档的形式）。

参考作答

1）Cognitive Constructivism

Cognitive constructivism（认知建构主义）与 social constructivism（社会建构主义）二者的差异：作为建构主义研究代表人物 Piaget 和 Vygotsky，二者的研究差异可以说明上述问题：Piaget 和 Vygotsky 是同一时期的学者，二者的研究虽然都与建构主义相关，但是其研究的方向并非一致。Piaget 的研究兴趣在于对认知及知识形成过程的探索，而 Vygotsky 却投身于研究社会及文化环境对人类学习所产生的影响。显然，后者更适用于教育领域，并且由于 Vygotsky 强调学习过程中社会及协作的本质，他也被称为社会建构主义学之父，而 Piaget 则被称为个人（认知）建构主义之父。

Amineh, R. J., & Asl, H. D. (2015). Review of constructivism and social constructivism. *Journal of Social Science, Literature and Languages, 1*(1), 9-16.

Abstract:

Although constructivism is a concept that has been embraced recently, a great number of sociologists, psychologists, applied linguists, and teachers have provided varied definitions of this concept. Also, many philosophers and educationalists such as Piaget, Vygotsky, and Perkins suggest that constructivism and social constructivism try to solve the problems of traditional teaching and learning. This research review represents the meaning and the origin of constructivism, and then discusses the role of leaning, teaching, learner, and teacher in the first part from constructivist perspective.

In the second part, the paper discusses the same issues, as presented in the first part, from social constructivist perspective. The purpose of this research review is to make EFL teachers and EFL students more familiar with the importance and guidance of both constructivism and social constructivism perspectives.

2）Zone of Proximal Development

(1) Wertsch, J. V. (1984). The zone of proximal development: Some conceptual issues. *New Directions for Child Development, 23*, 7-18.

Abstract:

This paper discusses Vygotsky's (1934 [1962]) ideas about the zone of proximal development (ZPD) and extends them by inclusion of the theoretical constructs of situation definition, intersubjectivity, and semiotic mediation. Vygotsky's notion of the ZPD has recently spurred much interest among developmental and cognitive psychologists. His ideas have been incorporated into studies on a variety of issues, including intelligence testing, memory, and problem solving. It is argued that several conceptual issues must be clarified to understand and use Vygotsky's insightful but somewhat cryptic claims about the ZPD. The fundamental theoretical construct that is needed in this connection is that of situation definition. It must be recognized that one and the same setting can be represented or defined in several different ways. Such notions as object representation and action pattern should be used to analyze situation definitions. It must also be recognized that in the ZPD, more than one situation definition is involved.

(2) Chaiklin, S. (2003). The zone of proximal development in Vygotsky's analysis of learning and instruction. In A. Kozulin, B. Gindis, V. Ageyev & S. Miller (Eds). *Vygotsky's educational theory and practice in cultural context* (pp.39-64). Cambridge University Press.

Abstract:

What kind of instruction is optimal for a particular child? Without doubt, this question is immediately comprehensible to any committed teacher in virtually any country in the world, and most of them are likely to want concrete answers to the question, not only as a theoretical puzzle, but in relation to their immediate practices. If one were to look to scientific psychology and educational research for advice in relation to this practical problem, what would the answer(s) look like? This simple question raises several profound problems. Normative and political issues about the goals of instruction and the resources available for realizing these goals must be resolved. A theory of learning is needed that can explain how intellectual capabilities are developed. If instruction is not viewed as an end in itself, then a theory about the relationship between specific subject-matter instruction and its consequences for psychological development is also needed. This last problem was the main tension against which Vygotsky developed his well-known concept of zone of proximal development, where the zone was meant to focus attention on the relation between instruction and development, while being relevant to many of these other problems. Vygotsky's concept of zone of proximal development is more precise and elaborated than its common reception or interpretation. The main purpose of this chapter is to provide a comprehensive introduction to and interpretation of this concept, along with comments about predominant contemporary interpretations. The chapter concludes with some perspectives and implications derived from the interpretation presented here.

3) Ecological Systems Theory

Ryan, D. P. J. (2001). Bronfenbrenner's Ecological Systems Theory. *Retrieved January, 9,* 2012.

Abstract:

This theory looks at a child's development within the context of the system of relationships that form his or her environment. Bronfenbrenner's theory defines complex "layers" of environment, each having an effect on a child's development. This theory has recently been renamed "bioecological systems theory" to emphasize that a child's own biology is a primary environment fueling her development. The interaction between factors in the child's maturing biology, her immediate family/community environment, and the societal landscape fuels and steers her development. Changes or conflict in any one layer will ripple throughout other layers. To study a child's development then, we must look not only at the child and her immediate environment, but also at the interaction of the larger environment as well.

4）Item Response Theory

(1) Van der Linden, W. J., & Hambleton, R. K. (1997). Item response theory: Brief history, common models, and extensions. In W. J. Linden & R. K. Hambleton (Eds.), *Handbook of modern item response theory* (pp.1-28). Springer New York.

Abstract:

Long experience with measurement instruments such as thermometers, yardsticks, and speedometers may have left the impression that measurement instruments are physical devices providing measurements that can be read directly off a numerical scale. This impression is certainly not valid for educational and psychological tests. A useful way to view a test is as a series of small experiments in which the tester records a vector of responses by the testee. These responses are not direct measurements but provide the data from which measurements can be inferred.

(2) Cai, L., Choi, K., Hansen, M., & Harrell, L. (2016). Item response theory. *Annual review of statistics and its application, 3*(1), 297-321.

Abstract:

This review introduces classical item response theory (IRT) models as well as more contemporary extensions to the case of multilevel, multidimensional, and mixtures of discrete and continuous latent variables through the lens of discrete multivariate analysis. A general modeling framework is discussed, and the applications of this framework in diverse contexts are presented, including large-scale educational surveys, randomized efficacy studies, and diagnostic measurement. Other topics covered include parameter estimation and model fit evaluation. Both classical (numerical integration based) and more modern (stochastic) parameter estimation approaches are discussed. Similarly, limited information goodness-of-fit testing and posterior predictive model checking are reviewed and contrasted. The review concludes with a discussion of some emerging strands in IRT research such as response time modeling, crossed random effects models, and non-standard models for response processes.

5）Task-based Interaction

(1) Seedhouse, P. (1999). Task-based interaction. *ELT Journal, 53*(3), 149-156.

Abstract:

The "task" has become a fundamental concept in language teaching pedagogy. However, there is a lack of studies which present a "holistic" analysis and evaluation of the interaction produced by tasks in the classroom. Based on a database of lesson extracts, this article attempts to characterize task-based interaction as a variety, discusses its pedagogical and interactional advantages and disadvantages, and considers what kinds of learning it might be promoting.

(2) Seedhouse, P., & Almutairi, S. (2009). A holistic approach to task-based interaction. *International Journal of Applied Linguistics, 19*(3), 311-338.

Abstract:

This paper proposes that interaction generated by tasks has previously been very difficult to analyse because of its highly indexical nature. Task-related actions and non-verbal communication could not be related easily to talk. A technological solution to this problem is presented, using a combination of task-tracking hardware and software, video recording and transcription. This enables a holistic approach, i.e., one in which all elements of behaviour can be integrated in analysis. Micro-analyses of multimodal data are undertaken, which provide revealing insights into the processes of task-based learning. A framework for describing and analyzing task-based interaction from a holistic perspective is outlined.

(3) Carless, D. (2002). Implementing task-based learning with young learners.

ELT Journal, 56(4), 389-396.

Abstract:

This article draws on qualitative classroom observation data from case studies of three EFL classes in Hong Kong primary schools. It analyses four themes relevant to the classroom implementation of task-based learning with young learners, namely, noise/indiscipline, the use of the mother tongue, the extent of pupil involvement, and the role of drawing or coloring activities. For each of these issues, strategies for classroom practice are discussed. It is suggested that the paper carries implications for teachers carrying out activities or tasks with young EFL learners in other contexts.

(4) Robinson, P. (2011). Task-based language learning: A review of issues. *Language Learning, 61*(1), 1-36.

Abstract:

Theoretically motivated, empirical research into task-based language learning has been prompted by proposals for task-based language teaching. In this review, I describe early and more recent proposals for how task-based learning can stimulate acquisition processes and the theoretical rationales that have guided research into them. I also describe taxonomies of task characteristics that have been proposed and claims made about the effects of task characteristics on interaction, attention to input, and speech production. I then relate the issues raised to findings described in the five empirical studies in this issue concerning the effects of pedagogic task design on the accuracy, fluency, and complexity of learner language; the influence of individual differences in cognitive and motivational variables on task performance; the extent to which tasks, and teacher interventions, promote the quantity and quality of interaction that facilitate L2 learning; and the generalizability of task-based learning research in laboratory contexts to instructed classroom settings.

6. 请用作者给出的 Task 的定义来审视自己理解和设计的教学任务 / 老师布置的教学任务有何异同？

参考作答 1

　　The authors define "task" as "the purposeful use of language to communicate personally significant meanings". There are three key points in this definition: "purposeful" "communicate" and "personally significant meaning". They remind me of some of my not-so-successful tasks assigned in my Chinese language class and inform me of what should be improved. The task designed should reflect what is learned in class (purposeful). It should serve "communicative purpose" (communicate), even though the tasks in class are only simulations of authenticity. It should also bring out what learners are thinking, not reciting (personally significant meaning).

参考作答 2

　　作者对 task 的定义为 an activity which leads to the purposeful use of language to communicate personally significant meanings。此定义中任务是用来引导有目的性地使用语言来进行一些有意义的交流活动。而我理解的 task 是课堂中设计的一个活动，通过不同的情境活动，学生可以进行不同的语言练习，更多地强调练习，并不是使用。教学任务就更不相同了，我设计的教学任务更像是这节课的教学目标，需要在这节课让学生学到什么知识和技能等，和文中的 task 含义相差甚远。

参考作答 3

　　作者给出 task 的定义时提到 "it leads to the purposeful use of language to communicate personally significant meanings"。首先可以肯定的是，不论是我们的 presentation 还是其他形式的教学任务，都符合前半段"有目的地使用语言"这个特征，但是可能对于后半部分"传达就个人而言重要的意义"这一部分做得还是不太够，很多教学任务的实用性和意义还不够且难度不符。

7. 请反思我们给学生的反馈 / 老师给你的反馈大都属于什么类型? 是否有效?

参考作答 1

Taking the subject of writing as an example, most of the feedback given or received by me in the past can be categorized as a corrective and summative type, which mainly focused on shallow learning and lacked the constructivist nature. Firstly, the students were not given the feedback of gap between the actual level and the reference level, or with no reference level or standard at all. Secondly, most of the feedback were about the corrections on choice of words, grammar or organization rather than the content, idea or meaning conveyed. Thirdly, teacher was the sole assessor, and peer feedback and self-evaluation were overlooked. Fourthly, teachers tended to grade students' writings or empower the students to grade their peers. However, previous studies indicated that both teacher's summative feedback (Knight & Yorke, 2003) and the grading by peers (Boud, 2000) were proved to be pernicious for effective learning. Lastly, the feedback provided lacked a feedforward nature. Due to the above reasons, our feedback seemed to be less effective.

References:

Boud, D. (2000). Sustainable assessment: rethinking assessment for the learning society. *Studies in continuing education*, *22*(2), 151-167.

Knight, P., & Yorke, M. (2003). *Assessment, learning and employability*. McGraw-Hill Education (UK).

参考作答 2

My supervisors provide me with written feedback on my writing and oral feedback on tutorials. They give critical and timely feedback on the place where I lack in-depth thinking, which usually elevates my thinking and argument to another level.

参考作答 3

认真回忆了一下自己的学习经历，对于反馈方面，我对两件事印象深刻。第一，大三上的写作课，当时我们有同伴反馈，大家就聚在一起讨论如何修改，并且要做一个同伴反馈情况的汇报；之后老师针对性地给出整体内容存在问题的口头反馈；我们交了终稿，老师给书面反馈没有给分数而是写评语；最后我们需要写反思报告。反馈周期挺长的，但是我一步一步做下来，真的在过程中有思考。第二，大二需要做一个写作课小组 presentation，当时我们都不知道该如何去做这个记叙文写作的展示，写作老师直接加入我们的群聊，给我们一对一及时的反馈，告诉我们如何去完善。老师和学生同时参与这个任务之后，学生得到非常专业的指导，也更有动力去做好这件事。我觉得这个很好地实现了任务里的互动和反馈。

参考作答 4

研究生阶段导师、课程老师给我的反馈主要分为书面反馈和口头反馈，前者一般体现在读书报告中，后者则多是 presentation 的口头当场反馈。这两种反馈都比较及时，所以我觉得都挺有效，区别在于书面反馈对我来说会更有帮助一些，因为可以反复查看相关反馈记录，同时留存得也更久一些。

8. 看完本章，你认为作者给出了"What is learning?"这个问题的答案吗？你能回答"What is learning?"这个问题吗？

参考作答 1

Their answer to "what is learning" has been woven in their arguments regarding learning theory, interaction and the role of teacher and student. From their perspectives, learning is considered a social activity in which students learn through task-based interactions with teachers and more capable peers. Learner's prior knowledge, criteria of success, scaffolding and pre-set goals all contribute to the learning process.

参考作答 2

作者从宏观角度对 What is learning 作出了相关的解释，如相关的学习理论、学习发生的条件，例如：interaction，teacher and student，但是作者没有对 learning 做名词解释。

关于 What is learning，我的回答基于前人文献和自身经验的定义，如学习是指经过强化练习后，个体行为潜能发生相对永久性变化的活动。但每个人对 learning 有自己不同的看法，所以对于这个问题的回答见仁见智。

9. 请重读 3.3.1 Tasks（pp.40–41），认真学习作者的研究与写作思路，并联系自己的研究与写作，看在哪些方面可以借鉴?

参考作答 1

The authors outline a number of definitions of task-based learning proposed by other researchers, stress their differences and propose their own definition that accords with the theme of this book. This is what proper academic writing should be like: informing readers about what has been proposed, then explaining your own ideas with supportive literature.

参考作答 2

作者先介绍了不同学者对于任务的不同定义，紧接着给出了自己对于这些定义的评价，最后提出自己对任务的定义。其实这样才能把以往的研究和自己现有的研究结合起来，评述起了桥梁作用。但是反思自身的学术写作，自己撰写的文献综述部分并没有成为整体不可或缺的部分，而且基本上只有述没有评。

10. 请读完本章第二遍后，尝试自己写本章的 summary。请重读 3.5 In summary (pp.54–55)，认真学习作者是如何将全章丰富却看似分散的信息 / 内容进行概括的。

参考作答 1

本章需要解决一个中心问题即"什么是学习"（"what is learning"）。作者基于对学习和形成性评价的相关文献的宏观回顾，引入了建构主义尤其是社会建构主义作为 LOA 模型发展的理论基础。同时作者对以学习为导向的课堂中尤为重要的基于任务的互动（task-based interactions）模式进行了介绍，其重要组成包括任务、教师辅助、目标、反馈等。最后作者还对老师和学生的角色进行了解释。作者希望 LOA 能够在任务连接下，增加课堂互动的有效性，帮助学生养成自我学习的习惯，同时能够促进其学习。作者的写作逻辑性很强，对相关概念的排序有自己的想法（相比较我可能更多的是按照章节中介绍的顺序来阅读），更加合理。

参考作答 2

作者首先指出"task"的重要地位，自然过渡到"什么是 task"的问题。作者对于"task"的概念进行了梳理，但需要注意到作者并非完全按照时间顺序进行——阐述，而是按照该研究领域对于该概念的认可程度按照从低到高进行排序，最后提及 Bygate 等的观点，强调学习者在目标解读与结果掌控方面的重要地位。这一观点与作者对"task"的定义具有共通性，作者定义的"task"——有目的地使用语言去交流个人的重要想法。在最后两段客观阐述对"task"定义的看法，承认其定义确有不足之处，但肯定了其总体方向是积极的。

作者在梳理文献时的排序方式及前后与上下文的自然过渡值得在今后的写作，尤其是文献综述的总结中借鉴运用。

第四章　什么是语言学习?
Chapter 4　What is language learning ?

章节目录

1. 思维导图呈现本章目录

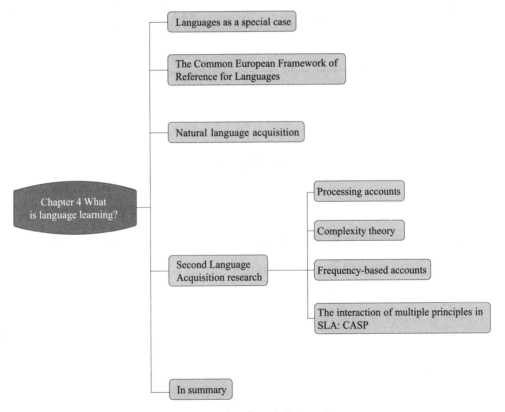

图 4.1　第四章思维导图目录

2. 表格呈现本章目录

表 4.1　第四章表格目录

4 What is language learning?	第四章 什么是语言学习？
LANGUAGES AS A SPECIAL CASE	4.1 语言作为一个特例
THE COMMON EUROPEAN FRAMEWORK OF REFERENCE FOR LANGUAGES	4.2 欧洲语言共同参考框架
NATURAL LANGUAGE ACQUISITION	4.3 自然语言习得
SECOND LANGUAGE ACQUISITION RESEARCH Processing accounts Complexity theory Frequency-based accounts The interaction of multiple principles in SLA: CASP	4.4 二语习得研究 4.4.1 过程描述 4.4.2 复杂理论 4.4.3 基于频次的描述 4.4.4 二语习得中多原则的相互作用：CASP
IN SUMMARY	4.5 小结

补充思考题及参考作答

1. 请翻译本章开始前引用的杜威的话（There's all the difference in the world between having something to say, and having to say something.）。请谈谈你对杜威这句话的理解，比如它与本章的关联或者对我们外语教或学的启示。

参考作答 1

　　学习正可谓是：有话可说直须言，莫逼无话找话说。这句话让我想到了一个概念即 motivation，无论在语言学习还是其他学习中，学生的主动性都是非常重要的，how to augment the motivation or say incentives for learning？同时联想到了之前看到的期望价值理论（Expectancy-value theory）中学生的"Do I want to do it ？" "Can I do it ？" 当这两项同时满足时，学习者会倾向于表现更好。我觉得这跟杜威这句话的描述有异曲同工之妙，积极主动地学习往往事半功倍。

参考作答 2

要说的和不得不说的，也就是自愿和非自愿的。联系到外语学习，应该是主张主动自愿地学习，对自己不愿意或者被迫做的事情往往做出来的东西都不会太令人满意。那么老师和学生自身其实可以激发学生自愿做事情的内驱力，自己主动做的事情，一般会取得不错的效果。

2. "Language is both the medium and the goal of learning." 请谈谈你对这句话的理解以及它如何体现语言学习的重要性。

参考作答 1

作者在文中对这句话有一定的解释，语言在教育中有几个重要的角色 "first language, foreign language and language of schooling"。首先语言本身无论是作为一语还是外语，都是学习的内容。而语言，不论是口语还是书面语都是传递知识的重要媒介，可以说是学习者必须要掌握的学习工具。本文作者特别强调 LOA 在语言学习中的重要性，因为语言学习更加强调 authentic learning，而 LOA 能够为学生创造更好的学习环境，其中的任务和反馈都能更好地促进学生学习。

参考作答 2

语言是学习的媒介以及目的。首先，语言是学习的媒介。在学习过程中，无论是语言学习还是其他学习，学习者都是基于语言获取知识。通过语言，学习者可以学习到语言所承载的学科思想、知识，以开阔眼界，深化认知。其次，语言学习本身属于学习的一种，因此语言学习也可谓是学习的目标。

3. 请查找和下载《欧框》2001 版的中英文和 2018 版 CEFR Companion Volume，尽可能浏览其内容，把它们作为教学和研究的重要参考文献。

参考作答

　　自 2001 年颁布以来，《欧洲语言共同参考框架：学习、教学、评估》（Common European Framework of Reference for Languages：Learning, Teaching, Assessment，以下简称《欧框》）对欧洲乃至世界范围内的语言学习、教学及评估等方面产生了深远的影响。作为一个多世纪以来欧洲语言教学理论及实践成果的系统总结，《欧框》的问世不仅具有划时代的里程碑意义（傅荣，2009），更指明了新世纪语言教学的发展方向（白乐桑、张丽，2008）。经过近二十载的推广与实践，《欧框》"已成为欧盟各国语言教学最有影响力的指导文件"（邹申 等，2015：24），同时也为欧盟以外国家或地区构建统一的语言能力测评体系提供了重要参考。

　　为了弥补《欧框》的不足，应对新时代的众多变化，欧洲理事会于 2014 年启动《欧框》扩展项目（Council of Europe 2018）。经过两年的调查研究与反复验证，欧洲理事会于 2016 年 10 月公布英法试行扩展版，向公众征询意见。2017 年 9 月，欧洲理事会先行推出经修改后的英文扩展版。2018 年 2 月，英法扩展版正式发布，再度引起了国内外语言教育界的关注（Piccardo et al.，2019；傅荣、李亚萌，2019；王正胜，2019）。

　　2018 年扩展版通过新增更多从零研制语言能力量表、增补描述语及更新描述表达，弥补了低龄阶段描述语欠缺、高级别描述语不充分、中介及多元语言与多元文化能力量表空白等方面的不足，大幅度扩展了《欧框》的语言能力描述框架，并新增手语能力等新的语言活动，使之能够适用于更为广泛的语言学习与教学环境，也有助于推动其语言教学理念与方法进一步走向世界。

　　《欧框》（扩展版）的推出对我国后续修订《中国英语能力等级量表》、完善《国际汉语能力标准》、探索多元化的语言教学体系具有参考价值，也可为日后有效整合汉语界、外语界与特殊教育领域的研究成果和资源，建立全国统一的语言能力框架提供借鉴。

4. 请查阅 5—10 篇 CEFR 的引介或综述及实证研究文献（如果是期刊文献，请查 SSCI & CSSCI 级别的文献）。请阅读其摘要，然后分享你的发现，或者分享你认为你的教与学中可以借鉴的地方。

参考作答 1

（1）查阅的中文期刊：

[1] 王正胜.《欧洲语言共同参考框架：学习、教学、评估（二）》解读 [J]. 外语测试与教学，2019（3）：19-24+59.

[2] 邹绍艳，金艳.《欧洲语言共同参考框架》写作能力量表的语境效度研究 [J]. 外语教学，2020（1）：34-39。

[3] 邹申，张文星，孔菊芳.《欧洲语言共同参考框架》在中国：研究现状与应用展望 [J]. 中国外语，2015，12（3）：24-31.

发现：查找的 3 篇中文 CEFR 相关的文献都是较新的，在介绍 CEFR 的同时很多文献都强调了其在中国语境下的实际运用，紧密联系了 CSE，展示了一段时间内的研究热点。更加启发我们思考怎样借鉴 CEFR 这个框架，如何促进 CSE 的相关修订？描述语和能力级别的难度是否匹配？怎样结合实际的大学英语教学与测试的实际需要推广 CSE，使其发挥应有的作用？

（2）查阅的英文期刊：

英文主要是浏览了 Cambridge English 第 63 期 Research Notes 中的几篇文章，关于量表本身，研究提出不同语境影响下更新 CEFR 描述语的必要性，以及需验证 CEFR 相关描述语，以期发挥更好的中介作用；也提到了该量表的运用，比如采用量表中描述语进行对比评价。

参考作答 2

[1]Ilc, G., & Stopar, A. (2014). Validating the Slovenian national alignment to CEFR: The case of the B2 reading comprehension examination in English. *Language Testing, 32*(4), 1-20.

[2]Chen, Y. H., & Baker, P. (2016). Investigating criterial discourse features across

second language development: Lexical bundles in rated learner essays, CEFR B1, B2 and C1. *Applied Linguistics*, *37*(6), 849-880.

[3] 刘建达，周艳琼.《实践中的欧洲语言共同参考框架》述评 [J].《外语教学与研究》，2017，49（4）：630-633.

[4] 王正胜.《欧洲语言共同参考框架：学习、教学、评估（二）》解读 [J].《外语测试与教学》，2019（3）：19-24+59.

[5] 邹申，张文星，孔菊芳.《欧洲语言共同参考框架》在中国：研究现状与应用展望 [J].《中国外语》，2015，12（3）：24-31.

发现：

"CEFR 对于欧洲语言教学产生了积极的作用，原因在于 CEFR 量表框架更多的是'能做'（can-do）描述语而不是词汇和语速等方面的定性要求，使得语言教师在具体教学中更容易理解和把握，从而更容易达成相关教学目标。而我国大学英语所依据的"教学大纲"或"课程要求"，对语言能力标准的描述除了有些定性的东西，主要是定量的。"（蔡基刚，2012）

根据自己的学习经历，我发现大部分老师在教学的时候都是注重词汇、语法等，少有关注学生的语言交际能力，导致目前大部分学生都是在听说方面存在较大问题。

此外，《欧框》一书大部分是针对成人教育的，对于低龄学习者没有举出相关的例子，所以未来我们还要关注低龄学习者的语言学习。

5. 请梳理和列出本章中的重要概念，对每一个概念请抄一遍专业的定义，并注明出处。请谈谈你在此过程中对这些概念是否有新的理解和新的发现。

参考作答

1）CEFR: The Common European Framework of Reference for Languages. The Framework provides a common basis for the elaboration of language syllabuses, curriculum guidelines, examinations, textbooks, etc. across Europe. It describes in a comprehensive way what language learners have to learn to do in order to use a language for communication and what knowledge and skills they have to develop so as to be able to act effectively. The description also covers the cultural context in which language is set. The Framework also defines levels of proficiency which allow learners' progress to be measured at each stage of learning and on a life-long basis (Council of Europe, 2001).

2）Action-oriented model: The approach adopted here, generally speaking, is an action-oriented one in so far as it views users sand learners of a language primarily as "social agents", i.e., members of society who have tasks (not exclusively language-related) to accomplish in a given set of circumstances, in a specific environment and within a particular field of action. While acts of speech occur within language activities, these activities form part of a wider social context, which alone is able to give them their full meaning. We speak of "tasks" in so far as the actions are performed by one or more individuals strategically using their own specific competences to achieve a given result. The action-based approach therefore also takes into account the cognitive, emotional and volitional resources and the full range of abilities specific to and applied by the individual as a social agent (European Council, 2001)

3）CASP model：As we pointed out in the Introduction we refer to our model as CASP, short for "Complex Adaptive System Principles of SLA", since it follows the general logic of complex adaptive systems (Gell-Mann, 1992). The model consists of four very general principles that we propose in this section.

The first general principle we propose is principle (A):

(A) Minimize Learning Effort (MiL)

Learners of a second language (L2) prefer to minimize learning effort when they learn the grammatical and lexical properties of the L2.

The second general principle is (B):

(B) Minimize Processing Effort (MiP)

Learners of a second language (L2) prefer to minimize processing effort when they use the grammatical and lexical properties of the L2, just as native speakers do.

This is captured in principle (C).

(C) Maximize Expressive Power (MaE)

Learners of a second language (L2) prefer to maximize their expressive power, i.e., to formulate in the L2 whatever thoughts they would wish to express in the L1, and to perform the same language functions as L1 users.

Principle (D)

(D) Maximize Communicative Efficiency (MaC)

Learners of a second language (L2) prefer to maximize their communicative efficiency in relation to the hearer and his/her mental model.

6. 请梳理和列出本章中提到的理论，对每一个理论请查阅至少一篇代表性著述 / 文献。请阅读并附上文献的摘要。请列一份文献目录，并在群里分享你的目录和查到的文献的 PDF 文件。

参考作答

1）Complexity Theory

Ellis, B. (2013). An overview of complexity theory: Understanding primary care as a complex adaptive system. In J. Sturmberg & C. Martin (Eds.), *Handbook of Systems and Complexity in Health* (pp.485-494). Springer.

Abstract:

This chapter introduces complexity theories and proposes that primary care can be thought of as a negotiated balance between imperfectly aligned and sometimes conflicting goals within a complex adaptive system (CAS). A CAS approach is interpreted as a framework that assists in thinking about the nature of primary care that allows consideration of its dynamic beyond the practice, the background of trend towards integrated organizations and federated models of practice. To illustrate how the propositions described can be put into daily practice the author brings in the literature on informatics relevant to quality improvement. The chapter concludes and makes recommendations in two key areas: education and learning to manage health information.

2）Input processing:

Van Patten, B. (2015). Input processing in adult second language acquisition. In B. VanPatten & J. Williams (Eds.), *Theories in second language acquisition: An introduction* (pp.113-134). Routledge.

Abstract:

Input Processing (IP) is concerned with the mistakes second language learners make in comprehension because acquisitions, to a certain degree, are a byproduct of comprehension. Although comprehension cannot guarantee acquisition, acquisition cannot happen if comprehension does not occur. Why? Because a good deal of acquisition is dependent upon learners making appropriate form-meaning connections during the act of comprehension. A good deal of acquisition is dependent upon learners correctly interpreting what a sentence means. In this chapter the author deals with the fundamentals of IP and the research associated with it. It will become clear that IP is not a comprehensive theory or model of language acquisition. Instead, it aims to be a model of what happens during comprehension that may subsequently affect or interact with other processes.

7. 请查阅 Filipovic, L. and Hawkins, J. A. (2013), 浏览全文，并谈谈你对 Figure 4.1 CASP general and specific principles 的理解。

参考作答

这篇文章中 Flilipovic 和 Hawkins 首先给出了 CASP 的全称，complex adaptive system principles，随后对二语习得中的一些重要概念进行了介绍，如 transfer and non-transfer，processing and learning，complexity and efficiency。接着，重点介绍了 CASP model，其中主要和具体的原则就是书上 Figure 4.1

CASP general and specific principles 的内容。首先看到 minimize 和 maximize 就想到认知的经济原则，简单来说人在交际时最小化努力，最大化效率，例如某些词汇、表达是比较简单的，我们就会用得更多，而不是费神去思考不常见的表达。这 和 Maximize Positive Transfer 中 "Properties of the L1 which are also present in the L2 are learned more easily and with less learning effort, and are readily transferred, on account of preexisting knowledge in L1" 的表达是一致的。我觉得 Figure 4.1 四者与学习者付出的学习努力紧密相连，有很强的内在联系。

8. 请浏览 English Profile Studies 的官网，了解这个系列的特色。

参考作答

1）English Profile is a collaborative program designed to enhance the learning, teaching and assessment of English worldwide. Its aim is to create a "profile" or set of Reference Level Descriptions for English linked to the Common European Framework of Reference for Languages (CEFR). These volumes summarise the latest research from the program.

2）Reference Level Descriptions：

The CEFR is language-neutral and operates across many different languages. To ensure that it can be fully adapted to local contexts and purposes, the Council of Europe has encouraged the production of Reference Level Descriptions (RLDs) for national and regional languages. RLDs provide detailed, language-specific guidance for users of the CEFR.

The English Profile Program has taken charge of this development for English. However, while the Council of Europe guidelines and the existing work of the T-series (Breakthrough, Waystage, Threshold, Vantage) take a "horizontal" approach, focusing on each level separately, English Profile follows a "vertical" approach: it concentrates on the description of linguistic ability in specific areas of the English language(vocabulary, grammar, language functions, etc.) across all six CEFR levels, using empirical data from learner corpora and curricula to inform its research findings.

The listing of vocabulary by level and category in the English Vocabulary Profile and the Can-Do statements in the English Grammar Profile are two outcomes of the English Profile Programmer's development of RLDs. Two other EPP initiatives have been published in book form within the English Profile Studies series and are relevant to the development of RLDs: Volume 1, Criterial Features in L2 Engl   Filipovic and Hawkins, discusses the distinguishing features of each CEFR   h and Volume 2, Language Functions Revisited by Green reviews l   ict definition across the ability range.

3）该系列共 7 卷

English Profile Studies Vol. 1: Criterial Features in L2 English

English Profile Studies Vol. 2: Language Functions Revisited

English Profile Studies Vol. 3: Immigrant Pupils Learn English

English Profile Studies Vol. 4: The CEFR in Practice

English Profile Studies Vol. 5: English Profile in Practice

English Profile Studies Vol. 6: Critical, Constructive Assessment of CEFR-informed Language Teaching in Japan and Beyond

English Profile Studies Vol. 7: The Discourse of the IELTS Speaking Test

This volume introduces a new concept, "criterial features", for the learning, teaching and testing of English as a second language. The work is based on research conducted within the English Profile Program at Cambridge University, using the Cambridge Learner Corpus.

The authors address the extent to which learners know the grammar, lexicon and usage conventions of English at each level of the CEFR. These levels are currently illustrated in functional terms with "Can Do" statements. Greater specificity and precision can be achieved by using the tagged and parsed corpus, which enables researchers to identify criterial features of the CEFR levels, i.e., Properties that are characteristic and indicative of L2 proficiency at each level. In practical terms, once criterial features have been identified, the grammatical and lexical properties of English can be presented to learners more efficiently and in ways that are appropriate to their levels.

4）Key features

Presents and analyses many illustrative criterial features taken from the current Cambridge Learner Corpus and linked to the proficiency levels of the CEFR.

Incorporates an unusually broad range of theoretical disciplines in the language sciences that inform the search for criterial features: second language acquisition, first language acquisition, language processing, language typology, computational linguistics, and grammatical theory.

Outlines a new multi-factor model of second language acquisition containing several interacting principles informed by current theories, published data and corpus findings.

Illustrates the practical benefits of criterial features for learning, teaching, textbook writing and syllabus design, publishing, and language assessment.

9. 请抄写或打印一遍本章的详细目录，包括每节中的 sub-headings。请谈谈你在梳理过程中是否有新理解和新发现。

参考作答

（1）目录整理

Chapter 4 What is language learning?

4.1 Language as a special case

4.2 The Common European Framework of Reference for Languages

4.3 Natural language acquisition

4.4 Second Language Acquisition research

    4.4.1 Processing accounts

4.4.2 Complexity theory

4.4.3 Frequency-based accounts

4.4.4 The interaction of multiple principles in SLA: CASP

4.5 In summary

（2）理解和发现：

本章节需要回答"什么是语言学习？"这一问题。作者首先对于语言学习相较于其他学习的特殊性进行阐述（背景介绍），侧重"语言"学习中的"语言"二字；然后以 2001 年出版的 CEFR 为例，说明了"什么是好的语言能力？"；在第三节中指出第一语言习得的过程，欲以此作为第二语言习得的借鉴方式；最后一部分对以上内容进行总结。

通过对作者的写作思路的梳理，有以下发现：1）回答"××是什么"首先需要对这一概念中的名词所涉及的特殊信息做一个说明；2）回答"××是什么"需要明确做 ×× 事情的目标及达成目标的方法；3）目标及方法的参照需要选取具有公信力的参照系。

10. 请按照本章中文献出现的先后顺序做一份本章的 References，重复的文献按顺序重复排列。请谈谈你在梳理过程中是否有新理解和新发现。

参考作答

1）本章参考文献目录

1.Dewey. J. (1915). *The School and Society*. Cosimo Classics.

2.Cumming, A. (2009). Language assessment in education: Test, curricular and teaching. *Annual Review of Applied Linguistics*, *29*, 90-100.

3.Coleman, J. A. (2004). Modern languages in British university: Past and present. *Arts and Humanities in Higher Education*, *3*(2), 295-317.

4.Davison, C., & Leung C. (2009). Current issues in English language teacher-based assessment. *TESOL Quarterly*, *43*(3), 393-415.

5.Weir, C. J. (2005b). *Language testing and validation: An evidence-based approach*. Palgrave.

6.Hawkins, J. A., & Filipovic, L. (2012). *Criterial features in L2 English: Specifying the reference levels of the Common European Framework,* English Profile Studies Volume 1. UCLS/Cambridge University Press.

7.Council of Europe. (2001). *Common European Framework of reference for languages: Learning, teaching, assessment*. Cambridge University Press.

8.Council of Europe. (2001). *Common European Framework of reference for languages: Learning, teaching, assessment*. Cambridge University Press.

9.VanPatten, B. (1996). *Input processing and grammar instruction*. Ablex.

10.VanPatten, B. (Ed) (2004). *Processing instruction: Theory, research and commentary*. Lawrence Erlbaum Associates.

11.VanPatten, B. (2007). Input processing in adult and second language acquisition, In B. Vanpatten & J. Williams (Eds.), *Theories in second language acquisition*. Lawrence Erlbaum Associates.

12.Vanpatten, B. (2008). Processing matters, In T. Piske & M. Young-Scholten (Eds.), *Input matters* (pp.113-134). Multilingual Matters.

13.Clahsen, H., & Felser, C. (2006). Grammatical processing in language learners. *Applied Psycholinguistics, 27*(1), 3-42.

14.Gass, S. M. (2003). Input and interaction. In C. J. Doughty & M. H. Long (Eds.), *Handbook of second language acquisition* (pp.224-225). Blackwell.

15.Klein, W. (1986). *Second language acquisition*. Cambridge University Press.

16.Truscott, J., & Sharwood-Smith, M. (2004). Acquisition by processing: A modular perspective on language development. *Bilingualism: Language and Cognition, 7*(1), 1-20.

17.Ellis, R. (1994). *The study of second language acquisition*. Oxford University Press.

18.Gass, S. M., & Selinker, L. (2008). *Second language acquisition: An introductory course* (3rd edition). Routledge.

19.Ellis, N. C. (1998). Emergentism, connectionism and language learning. *Language Learning, 48*(4), 631-664.

20.Gell-Mann, M. (1992). Complexity and complex adaptive system. In J. A. Hawkins & M. Gell-mann (Eds.), *The evolution of human languages* (pp.3-18). Addison-Wesley.

21.Larsen-Freeman, D. (1997). Chaos/complexity science and second language acquisitions. *Applied Linguistics, 18*(2), 141-165.

22.Larsen-Freeman, D., & Cameron, L. (2008). *Complex systems in applied linguistics.* Oxford University Press.

23.O'Grady, W. (2005). *Syntactic carpentry: An emergentist approach to syntax.* Lawrence Erlbaum Associates.

24.Larsen-Freeman, D. (2012). Complexity Theory. In S.M. Gass & A. Mackey (Eds.), *The Routledge handbook of second language acquisition.* Routledge.

25.Lee, N., & Schumann, J. (2005). The international instinct: The evolution and acquisition of language, paper presented at AILA, Madison, Wisconsin.

26.Larsen-Freeman, D. (2012). Complexity Theory. In S.M. Gass, & A. Mackey. (Eds), *The Routledge handbook of second language acquisition* (pp.73-87). Routledge.

27.Evans, J. (2007). The emergence of language: A dynamical systems account. In E. Hoff & M. Shatz (Eds.), *Handbook of language development* (pp.128-147). Blackwell.

28.Larsen-Freeman, D. (2012). Complexity theory. In S.M. Gass & A. Mackey (Eds.), *The Routledge handbook of second language acquisition* (pp.73-87). Routledge.

29.Larsen-Freeman, D. (2012). Complexity theory. In S.M. Gass & A. Mackey (Eds.), *The Routledge handbook of second language acquisition* (pp.73-87). Routledge.

30.Saussure, F. D. (1916). *Cours de linguistique generale.* Duckworth.

31.James, W. (1890). *The principles of Psychology.* Holt.

32.Saussure, F. D. (1916). *Cours de linguistique generale.* Duckworth.

33.Saussure, F. D. (1916). *Cours de linguistique generale*. Duckworth.

34.Ellis, N. C. (2012). Frequency-based accounts of second language acquisition. In S.M. Gass & A. Mackey. A (Eds.), *The Routledge handbook of second language acquisition* (pp.193-210). Routledge.

35.Ellis, N. C. (2012). Frequency-based accounts of second language acquisition. In S.M. Gass & A. Mackey (Eds.), *The Routledge handbook of second language acquisition* (pp.193-210). Routledge.

36.Gell-Mann, M. (1992). Complexity and complex adaptive system. In J. A. Hawkins & M. Gell-mann (Eds.), *The evolution of human languages* (pp.3-18). Addison-Wesley.

37.Hawkins, J.A., & Gell-mann, M. (Eds) (1992). *The evolution of human languages*. Addison-Wesley.

38.Larsen-Freeman, D. (1997). Chaos/complexity science and second language acquisitions. *Applied Linguistics*, *18*(2), 141-165.

39.Filipovic, L., & Hawkins, J. A. (2013). Multiple factors in second language acquisition: The CASP and model. *Linguistics*, *51*(1), 145-176.

40.Hawkins J. A., & Buttery, P. (2009). Using learner language from corpora to profile levels of proficiency: Insights from the English Profile Programme. In L. Taylor & C. J. Weir (Eds.), *Language testing matters: Investigating the wider social and educational impact of assessment,* Studies in Language Testing, Volume 31 (pp.158-175). UCLES/Cambridge University Press.

41.Hawkins, J. A., & Filipovic, L. (2012). *Criterial features in L2 English: Specifying the reference levels of the common european framework,* English Profile Studies, Volume 1. UCLS/Cambridge University Press.

2）发现：

（1）在本章节所涉及的41个参考文献中，有14个参考文献是由两人或以上合作完成的。有些作者不限于和一个人合作，而是与多人合作，如Hawkins就曾与Filipovic、Buttery或Gell-mann分别合作过。说明学术研究中合作和交流是非常必要的。

（2）在本章节的引用文献中，被引用次数较高的学者有 Gass（9 次，但多数是间接引用，猜测 Gass 的重要地位出现较早）、Larsen-Freeman（7 次）、Hawkins（6 次）、Vanpatten（4 次）、Filipovic（3 次）、Saussure（3 次）和 Ellis（3 次）。以上学者的文献对于进一步了解"什么是语言学习？"有重要启发作用，可以将以上学者在本章节中的参考著述列入待学习书单中。

（3）通过观察，发现每位学者的著述都有重复率较高的关键词，如 Larsen-Freeman（complexity theory），Hawkins（evolution/assessment），大致可以判断每位学者研究的具体领域。对于以后针对某一方面的深入学习找到了可参读的学者及其著述。

（4）本章节参考文献的时间跨度从 1890 年至 2013 年，但 1890 年的仅有一篇，文献的出版时间大多集中在 20 世纪 90 年代至 21 世纪，中间几乎没有间断。说明对于"什么是语言学习"的研究从 20 世纪 90 年代至今持续受到关注。

第五章　要学习什么?
Chapter 5　What is to be learned？

章节目录

1. 思维导图呈现本章目录

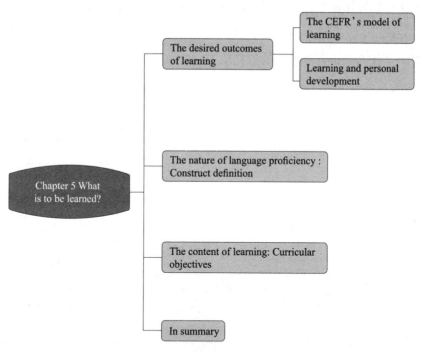

图 5.1　第五章思维导图目录

2. 表格呈现本章目录

表 5.1 第五章表格目录

5 What is to be learned?	第五章 要学习什么?
THE DESIRED OUTCOMES OF LEARNING The CEFR's model of learning Learning and personal development	5.1 预期的学习结果 5.1.1 欧框的学习模型 5.1.2 学习和个人发展
THE NATURE OF LANGUAGE PROFICIENCY	5.2 语言水平的本质
THE CONTENT OF LEARNING: CURRICULAR OBJECTIVES	5.3 学习内容:课程目标
IN SUMMARY	5.4 小结

补充思考题及参考作答

1. 你认为什么样的学习才算是"成功的学习"? 为什么?

参考作答 1

我很欣赏社会建构主义的观点,学习的目的是"enable students to continue learning throughout life",这和本章开篇杜威名言"enable individuals to continue their learning"完全契合。

我认为成功的学习者具有成长型思维、有效的学习方法以及持续性学习的习惯。成功的教育是使个人能够终身学习,给予学习者更加广阔的视野,让他们看到外面的世界。这个外面的世界可能让他看到和他原本世界的差异性与多样性,也可能让他意识到自己的不足,进而培养开放的心态与成长的思维,他才会主动去接触学习的环境,调动身边的学习资源,这就让学习者有了目标意识。有了方向后,他还需要知道达到目标的方法。虽然方向各有不同,到达的路径也不同,但实质都是遇到问题—分析问题—解决问题。所以在学习中应该培养学习者解决问题和克服困难的能力。最后通过微小积累，持续改变。所以"成功的学习"让学习者在人生道路上能较为出色地回答"我去哪儿"和"我怎么去"的问题。

参考作答 2

　　成功的学习应该能够使自己成为一个终身学习者，具有对知识的渴望，并发展出健全的人格，就像作者说的，"A very positive outcome of learning would thus be that students acquire the valuable dispositions and life skills that enable them to continue learning throughout life."

参考作答 3

　　我认为当把学习变成一种习惯时，就算是"成功的学习"。因为，当学习变成了一种习惯，那么学习就是主动的、有方向的和有目标的。每一处学到的知识都能连接起来，最后形成一张知识网。现在不要认为你学到的东西好像没有什么用处，其实在未来生活或工作某一处你会有所顿悟，你会将所学的知识运用于生活或工作中，这就来源于你之前学过的知识。学习本身就是一个提升自我、锤炼自我的过程，学习就是一场修行。

2. 你认为如何才能成为一名"优秀的语言学习者"？为什么？

参考作答 1

　　As successful language learners understand, each language learned to a good level adds a new dimension to their view of themselves and how they relate to and act in the world. How to be a successful language learner could do as follows. At first, to learn according to school curriculum and construct self-cognitive knowledge system. Second, to cultivate independent creative activity competence and cognitive competence. Third, to measure basic competence in workplace and achieve the valuable dispositions and life skills. Fourth, to learn advanced thinking in higher order according to social requirements.

参考作答 2

成为"优秀的语言学习者",会让这门语言融入血液,成为身体不可或缺的一部分。首先,要有对语言学习的热爱,有爱才会真心付出;其次,要有韧性,学习一门语言并不是一件容易的事,非要有毅力和韧性不可。要做优秀的语言学习者那更需要持之以恒,下苦功夫;再次,优秀的语言学习者要有钻研的精神,语言的内涵非常丰富,包含有历史、社会、文化、心理等诸多方面,这些都需要有执着的精神去探索;最后,优秀的语言学习者,能够引领大家一起学习,共同学习,我觉得幸老师便是最好的榜样。

参考作答 3

一名优秀的语言学习者应该 1)learning how to learn; 2)通过学习语言,培养自己对目标语文化的喜爱(One outcome of becoming a good language learner is to develop an affinity with the culture where the language is spoken.)。这两点为学习者提供不断追求卓越的源泉和动力。

参考作答 4

首先,成为一名"优秀的语言学习者"的前提,是自己要精通一门语言,比如自己的母语。因为只有在精通一门语言后,学习者才有可能对其他语言有更深的感知能力,才有可能理解语言的精妙之处。

其次,学习者要会善用类比,找到目的语和母语之间的区别与联系,用已知去探索未知。

再次,学习者在学习新知识的同时,要经常巩固复习。

最后,学习者应将学到的语言运用起来,将语言融入自己的生活。

3. L1 学习者与 L2 学习者需要掌握的 "skill" 有何区别？为什么？这对我们的外语教学或学习有何启示？

参考作答 1

"Skill" in L1 focuses on purpose-driven communication, which figures as the lowest level, reflecting a "belief that writing consists of applying knowledge of a set linguistic patterns and rules for sound-symbol relationships and sentence construction". The term in L2 is used to identify competences which have value in society. It is understood as higher-order, emergent outcomes of learning.

In language teaching, we need to know how to set the curricular objectives between L1 and L2 because of their different levels and goals. And the duty of our teaching is not just to teach the basic knowledge in school curriculum. Practical, social, and professional competences are more important to merge into the socio-cognitive construct.

参考作答 2

1) The difference of skills:

In L2: skill is used to identify competences which have value in society. It collocated easily with adjectives like "practical" "social" or "professional". These are also the competences in CEFR's action-oriented model of learning. Language competence develops through social interaction to serve social purposes—the social cognitive model. In the second language context, "skills" are understood as the higher-order, emergent outcomes of learning.

In L1: "skill" figures as the lowest level, then come creativity, process, genre, social practices, and sociopolitical discourse. The reason for this difference is obvious: In L1 for most pupils the language as a system is already effectively mastered, so that all discourses are potentially available, and to focus on the low-level mechanisms of written text is to ignore or assume all the higher-level ones. Thus "skills" refer to the basic understanding of sound-symbol relationships etc. upon which higher levels are based.

2）原因：

二者之所以有此区别是因为二者的学习过程和目标不同。"skill"在 L1 中被定义为初级技能，因为在此过程中，涉及的是声音和符号关系的基本理解，不涉及社会认知的建构及个人的发展；在 L2 中，"skill"的获得需要通过基于行动的学习来建构社会认知模型，在此过程中实现积极的性情、态度和自我形象的建构。因此，这个过程是一种高级的学习形式。

3）启示：

外语教学作为一种 L2 学习，要注重对学习者高阶能力的培养。如果能将语言学习与社会认知的建构及个人的发展融合起来，那么语言学习的过程就是一种高阶能力的培养过程。

4. 结合教学或学习实践，你认为应该如何设定一门课程的教学目标？为什么？

参考作答 1

The curricular objectives should: a) align with external assessment; b) identify the higher-order outcomes of learning; c) concern the content of learning, its presenting method and sequence; and d) define teacher's to-do list.

参考作答 2

课程的教学目标首先应基于培养方案或教学大纲，课程要达到培养方案中的设定目标。然后，课程的教学目标设置也要遵循国家的政策导向、学生的需求和社会需求。因为学习是为了学习者自身的发展，同时也需要面向社会为国家培养人才。只有将课程的教学目标放在整个人才培养方案里面，才能形成整体的育人体系。

以英语精读课为例，教学目标的设定，应从培养方案、教学大纲、语言知识、语言能力、个人发展五个方面来设定。

参考作答 3

设定一门课程的教学目标通常会根据课程标准去设定。课程标准有些在学校层面，有些在更高层面，比如市、省，甚至国家层面。通常教学目标的设定是为了达到一个特定标准，因此这个标准的选定很重要，只有先选定了课程标准，才能根据课程标准去设定教学目标。

而后在课程标准的指导下，结合课程内容，确定教学重点。在这个过程中，还要结合学生的现状，确定难点所在，重点和难点的确定即教学目标的确定。

以语言课程为例，作为 L2，根据 CASP 的原则，学习要考虑经济效益的问题。因为时间是有限的，如何在有限的时间中达到好的学习效果，是教学目标设定时需要考虑的重要原则。

5. 为什么作者要花大篇幅写第 3—5 章？这三章与 LOA 有何关联？

参考作答 1

为了阐释不同层次的测评是如何共同促进学习的，第 3—5 章提出了 LOA 涉及的三个基本问题：什么是学习？什么是语言学习？要学习什么？

第三章从个体认知的角度介绍了建构主义和社会建构主义，为 LOA 提供了较为合理的理论模型。本章强调任务和教师在鼓励学习者互动方面的重要性，指出这种做法可以提高课堂评价的效果。

由于 LOA 与学习紧密相关，语言学习是 LOA 的目标，同时也是学习的中介，所以第四章将主题聚焦到教育的特殊案例——语言。通过运用《欧框》这一基于行动的案例，本章主要讨论学习者语言能力的发展。此外，本章还引出第一语言和第二语言的学习过程，以加深读者对社会—认知（Socio-cognitive）模式下学习的整体理解。

第五章聚焦正规教育背景下语言学习的组织，讨论学习的三个方面：社会期待的结果、需要掌握的技能（社会—认知建构）和学习的内容（课程内容）。本章"技能"（skill）一词在第一语言学习中被解释为初级机制（entry-level mechanism），而在第二语言学习中则被解释为高级能力（higher-order competence）。

参考作答 2

　　LOA 是面向学习的测评，因此作者首先在第二章先介绍了 LOA 的源起和发展，第 3—5 章都是介绍和学习相关的内容。第 3 章 What is learning 为 LOA 提供了较为合理的理论模型，第 4 章 What is language learning 正式提出了 LOA 研究的主要领域是在语言学习，第 5 章 What is to be learned 则讨论了学习的三个方面，对这些问题的理解能使读者更好地进行以下几章的阅读。这三章介绍了学习及语言学习的方方面面，为后面做铺垫，接下来的章节介绍面向学习的测评。

参考作答 3

　　第 3—5 章分别讲述了学习的三个基本问题，即什么是学习，什么是语言学习以及要学习什么。这三章与 LOA 有着紧密的联系。第 3 章从个体认知的角度介绍建构主义和社会建构主义，为 LOA 提供了较为合理的理论模型，并指出任务可以促进交互的产生，在面向学习的测评中发挥重要作用。教师与学生分享任务成功的标准，并鼓励学生积极参与互动，帮助学生在完成任务中获得能力，这一做法有助于提高课堂评价的效果。第 4 章指出了语言学习是 LOA 的目标。作者通过阐述复杂理论的主张，讨论学习者语言能力的发展，引出第一语言和第二语言的学习过程，以加深对社会—认知模式下学习的理解。同时强调外语教学是动态学习的管理过程，教师的教与学生的学要相吻合。第 5 章从社会期待的结果、社会—认知建构和课程目标设置三个方面进一步探讨语言学习。作者指出在社会建构主义视角下，学习不仅需要获取学科知识，更需要养成独立的创新能力和认知能力，促进个人的发展，形成终身学习的品格。读者通过这三章的阅读，获取了对于学习，尤其是语言学习在社会建构主义下的诠释和理论，为第 6—8 章探讨测评在学习中的角色和 LOA 在课堂中扮演的角色做好理论铺垫。

参考作答 4

从本书的主题 Learning Oriented Assessment 可以看出，learning 是核心词，因此需要了解与学习有关的内容：即 What，How，Why 三个方面。而第 3—5 章，分别从什么是学习，到什么是语言学习，学什么，来解释学习的 What，How，Why。从学习到语言学习，是从一般到特殊的过程，先让读者了解学习的本质，再到语言学习的本质，层层深入。语言学习到学什么内容，则是从理论到实践。从方法到内容，最终把学习、语言学习所倡导的有效理论落实到语言学习的内容上，体现 Learning Oriented 的理念。

参考作答 5

LOA 是面向学习的测评，只有叙述清楚学习是什么、语言学习的特殊性、语言学习该学什么等一系列问题之后，才能讨论如何面向学习开展测评。

第六章 大规模测评在学习中的作用
Chapter 6 The role of large-scale assessment in learning

章节目录

1. 思维导图呈现本章目录

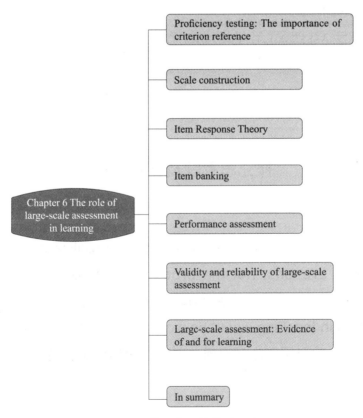

图 6.1 第六章思维导图目录

2. 表格呈现本章目录

表 6.1　第六章表格目录

6 The role of large-scale assessment in learning	第 6 章 大规模测评在学习中的作用
PROFICIENCY TESTING: THE IMPORTANCE OF CRITERION REFERENCE	6.1 水平测试：标准参照在学习中的重要性
SCALE CONSTRUCTION	6.2 量表开发
ITEM RESPONSE THEORY	6.3 项目反应理论
ITEM BANKING	6.4 题库
PERFORMANCE ASSESSMENT	6.5 表现评价
VALIDITY AND RELIABILITY OF LARGE-SCALE ASSESSMENT	6.6 大规模测评的信度和效度
LARGE-SCALE ASSESSMENT: EVIDENCE OF AND FOR LEARNING	6.7 大规模测评：以评测学和以评促学
IN SUMMARY	6.8 小结

补充思考题及参考作答

1. 请翻译杜威的名句（Were all instructors to realize that the quality of mental process, not the production of correct answers, is the measure of educative growth something hardly less than a revolution in teaching would be worked.）。你如何理解这句话里时态的使用？此引用与本章有何关联？对我们教学有何启示？

参考作答 1

翻译：如果所有的老师都能意识到衡量教育水平发展的标尺并非获得正确答案，而是如何保证思维过程的质量，那么教育的发展不亚于一场教学革命。

语气：这句话里的"Were，would be worked"是将来时态的一种虚拟语气形式，"is the measure of"这里用一般现在时表示的是一种客观事实或真理。

关联：本章讲的是大规模测评在学习中的作用，我们需要思考测评的目的是什么？是追求结果和通过率还是通过测评这个手段来反观学生的学习能力，特别是学生思维训练过程的质量和有效性，这些和作者所提及的这句话息息相关。

启示：在教学中，应该注重学生的思维训练，如批判分析能力（critical thinking），让他们多提问题，凡事不仅要知其然，还要知其所以然。导读的这种自己先读、自己提问、相互提问、老师提问；自我解答、相互解答、老师点评反馈的方式其实就是一种很好的思维训练的方式。

参考作答 2

翻译：如果所有的教育者都能够意识到思维过程的质量——而不是产出正确答案——才是衡量教育进步的标准该多好啊，其价值不亚于一场教育革命。

时态：该句中虚拟语气 were...would be 的使用说明此句内容还是作者的一种期待和设想而不是现实。

关联：此句与本章的关系主要体现在作者通过本章的观点验证了杜威的这句名句，也是通过这句话为本章提供支撑。本章阐述通过大规模测评促进取得更好的学习效果，这既是一种促进思维的过程，也是促使教育者反思的过程。同时本章提供的思路对教学和评估具有重要的借鉴意义。

启示：在教学中作为教育者，我们自己不仅要转变思维，而且要乐于实践。特别分享一点我今天上课的感悟。本来我今天要检查学生是否完成了上次布置的作业，但是上课前浏览了辜老师的点评，我临时改变教学设计，没有直接去检查完成情况，而是把作业变成不同的讨论题，启发学生来给出自己的回答。有些同学用到了作业中学习到的内容，有些同学在此过程中提出了疑问，有些同学回答了其他同学的疑问。在此过程中，我引导学生重点关注比较能够促进思考的问题，鼓励同学拓宽思路，或者追问他们有没有新的解决方案，最后我们不但完成了课程目标，学生们的思维也活跃起来。课上提出的好多问题，学生们自己就解决了。对于学生总体存在的问题，我也进行了引导，如引导他们看本章相关讲解，能不能解答他们的疑问，最后问题也解决了。整节课，他们更多的是在思考，而不是要找出正确答案。这是一种简单的实践，但是在此过程中，我感觉自己很有存在的价值，我知道自己想要做什么，我知道这对学生会有什么样的帮助，而学生们也不知不觉参与其中。期待他们慢慢把这种思考的学习方式变成习惯，进而变成一种能力。当然，如果我有充足的时间提前策划一下，效果应该会更好。其实，我最后应该再有针对性地留出新的思考任务，由于临时策划，这一点疏忽了，下次要提前做好准备。

参考作答 3

翻译：如果所有的教师都意识到，衡量学习者成长的尺度是思维过程的质量，而不是正确答案的产生，那么教育的发展将会带来一场教学革命。

语气：前半句话用的是虚拟语气，表示一个假设的情况，说明用思维过程的质量来衡量学习者的提升现在仍然不是一个真实情况，后半句用的一般现在时，说明把正确答案作为教育提升更接近于目前的状况。

关联：此处的引用表明本章主要讲的是大规模测评在学习中的角色，以及其信度和效度的保障等，测试工具的使用如何衡量学生所取得的成就或者教育所取得的成就。也正是引用中所提到的观点。

启示：教育者更应该把教育作为培养学生思维习惯的一种方式，而不仅仅是为了学生取得高分。在教学过程中应该着重培养他们的思维，而不是应试能力。作为学生，我们也应该着重于提高自己的学习和思维能力，而不仅仅是为了取得高分。

参考作答 4

翻译：如果所有的教师都意识到衡量受教育者成长的标准是思维过程的质量，而不是正确答案的产生，那么在教学方面，几乎可以说不亚于一场革命。

语气：这句话里用了虚拟语气，与实际情况相反，表示事实上教师们并没有这样的认识，现实中教育重视的是学生能够做出正确答案。

关联：这句话与第六章有紧密的联系。此句的引用是因为本章主要介绍了大规模测评在学习中的作用，包括一些很重要的概念，如信度、效度的保障，以及项目反应理论等，这些工具或者手段如何用来衡量学生的成就和发展或者教育的发展，这和杜威所提到的 measure of educative growth 可以进行关联。

启示：要在过程中多注重思考，如老师所说，要掌握做事的方法，而不仅仅能够做出来几道题。同时在学习过程中要注重培养思维能力，训练自己的批判性思维和创造性思维。

2. 请整理本章中的重要概念，并查阅专业词典，如我们之前推荐的外研社引进的《语言测试词典》。

参考作答

以下概念的解释均来自《语言测试词典》。

1）Proficiency：

A. A general type of knowledge of or competence in the use of a language, regardless of how, where or under what conditions it has been acquired.

B. Ability to do something specific in the language, for example, proficiency in English to study in higher education in the UK, proficiency to work as a foreign language teacher of a particular language in the United States, proficiency in Japanese to act as a tour guide in Australia.

C. Performance as measured by a particular testing procedure. Some of these procedures are so widely used that levels of performance on them (e.g., "superior" "intermediate" "novice" on the FSI scales) have become common currency in particular circles as indicators of language proficiency.

2）Proficiency test：

A test which measures how much of a language someone has learned. Unlike an achievement test, a proficiency test is not based on a particular course of instruction. A proficiency test often measures what the candidate has learned relative to a specific real-world purpose, for example, does he / she know enough of the target language to follow a lecture, train as an engineer or work as a ski instructor in that medium, or to translate to the requisite standard out of that language. Some proficiency tests have been standardized for worldwide use, such as the American TOEFL test which is used to measure the English language proficiency of foreign college students who wish to study in the USA; or the British-Australian IELTS test designed for those who wish to study in the UK or Australia. In spite of their worldwide standardization, proficiency tests normally have a particular situation in mind. TOEFL is primarily relevant to those who wish to study in the USA and its use of American English is therefore justifiable. Established proficiency tests such as the TOEFL or the Cambridge examinations tend to generate a washback effect on instruction and hence come more and more to be used as achievement tests. This achievement-proficiency dynamic rightly leads to new proficiency tests being designed.

3）Validity:

The quality which most affects the value of a test, prior to, though dependent on, reliability. A measure is valid if it does what it is intended to do, which is typically to act as an indicator of an abstract concept (for example height, weight, time, etc.) which it claims to measure. The validity of a language test therefore is established by the extent to which it succeeds in providing an accurate concrete representation of an abstract concept (for example proficiency, achievement, aptitude).

The most commonly referred to types of validity are:

Content; construct; concurrent; predictive

4）Reliability:

Also test reliability.

The actual level of agreement between the results of one test with itself or with another test. Such agreement, ideally, would be the same if there were no measurement error, which may arise from bias of item selection, from bias due to time of testing or from examiner bias. These three major sources of bias may be addressed by corresponding methods of reliability estimate:

Source of Bias	Reliability Estimate
1. selection of specific items	a. parallel forms
	b. split-half
	c. rational equivalence
2. time of testing	test-retest
3. examiner bias	inter-rater reliability checks

3. 请用测评的 basic process (p. 78) 自评我们的教学实践，哪些环节做得不够甚至缺失？如何改进？

参考作答 1

文中对测评的 basic process 描述为 "they are centered on tasks, which produce language activity, in conditions enabling observation and learning. These conditions include an appropriate level of challenge, comprehensible input and scaffolding which makes the task accessible. Feedback is generated, enabling performance to be evaluated."

导读实践活动基本都包含了这些过程，以思考题（自提或老师提）为任务，产生相应的读书报告。这些思考题具有挑战性，需要我们阅读该书和相关文献，同时借助老师和同学提供的帮助以及最后老师的反馈来完成。我觉得整体是比较完整的，于我个人而言则是未用英文回答，可以锻炼自己的写作能力；有时候思考题也做不完，要在之后再次阅读的时候进行相应的改正。

参考作答 2

在学习的过程中发现，observation 这个环节也许是需要改进的。老师不应该是单纯地批改作业或者不批改作业，对于学生是如何完成这个 task 的过程其实是不那么关注的。Comprehensible input 也是需要改进的，应该加大输入。学生应该多阅读一些自己能够理解的东西，只有理解了之后才会有输出。

4. 请下载和阅读 Broadfoot & Black（2004）文献 Redefining assessment，谈谈你对他们此话的理解（Educational assessment must be understood as a social practice, an art as much as a science, a humanistic project with all the challenges this implies）。推荐李筱菊教授的《语言测试科学与艺术》（湖南教育出版社 2001 版）。

参考作答 1

The completion of the first ten years of this journal is an occasion for review and reflection. The main issues that have been addressed over the ten years are summarized in four main sections: Purposes, International Trends, Quality Concerns and Assessment for Learning. Each of these illustrates the underlying significance of the themes of principles, policy and practice, which the journal highlights in its subtitle. The many contributions to these themes that the journal has published illustrate the diversity and complex interactions of the issues. They also illustrate that, across the world, political and public pressures have had the effect of enhancing the dominance of assessment so that the decade has seen a hardening, rather than any resolution, of its many negative effects on society. A closing section looks ahead, arguing that there is a move to rethink more radically the practices and priorities of assessment if it is to respond to human needs rather than to frustrate them.

参考作答 2

原文中此处解释了 *Assessment in Education* 期刊的特点是将测评放在不同的社会语境下考虑，其中测试对象、测试内容、测试目的和测试方法等都反映了不同社会语境（例如不同的时间和地点安排）。因此，文章作者在此处再次强调 educational assessment 的社会性，要兼顾科学的公正性和潜在的人的因素。这和 socio-constructivism 的理念有相似之处，同时测试的社会学转向也是我们必须要重点关注的。

参考作答3

　　"教育评估必须要作为一种社会实践,一项艺术,就像一门科学一样,这是一个充满挑战的人文主义项目"。教育评估要置于整个社会框架内,以建构主义和社会建构主义为指导,服务于现实社会,是作为一种社会实践而不仅仅是一种评估手段,这项人文主义项目也面临着很多挑战。面对这些挑战,需要解决的是思维问题,这也是首要的问题。

5. 请翻译 Messick(1989)对效度的定义:"An overall evaluative judgment of the degree to which evidence and theoretical rationales support the adequacy and appropriateness of interpretations and actions based on test scores"(p. 86),并谈谈你对此的理解。

参考作答1

　　翻译:对经验证据和理论依据在多大程度上支持分数的解释与使用进行的综合评价就是效度。

　　理解:以 Samuel Messick 为代表的研究者把效度看作一个整体概念,即整体效度概念(unitary concept of validity)。效度不再是某个单一的概念,也不再专注于区分各种类型的效度,而是应当从各个方面尽可能地收集证据,运用不同的测量手段来保证测试的结果能够得到合理的使用(邹申,2012)。效度验证现在需要进行更加综合全面的考虑,因为考试,特别是大规模考试不得不考虑其反拨效应。

参考作答2

　　翻译:对经验证据和理论依据在多大程度上支持分数的解释与使用进行的综合评价就是效度。

　　理解:有关效度的定义包含四个方面的信息:经验证据和理论依据、测试分数、充分合理的解释和行动、全面的评估判断。首先,需要了解什么样的经验证据和理论依据可以用来评估效度；其次，测试分数是指大规模测试的分数，然后需要弄清楚充分合理的解释的范畴，最后全面地评估判断包含的内容。这些都需要明确之后才能进行行之有效的效度研究。

6. 请重读本章对 Weir(2005) Socio-cognitive validity framework 的介绍（pp.88-89）。推荐阅读本人国家社科基金重点项目申报书"基于证据的大学英语四六级、雅思、托福考试效度对比研究"，并谈谈你的理解与收获。

参考作答 1

之前读过辜老师的国家社科基金重点项目申报书。写得很好，结构清楚，可以作为各类课题申报书的范本，但内容方面当时读不懂。今天再读，内容好像有些明白了，可能是因为近期在接触测试学的内容。这次再读，感觉申报书逻辑清楚，观点明确，每一个概念都做了简洁而清楚的阐述，一看就很明白要做的是什么，为什么这么做以及如何开展。

第一部分国内外研究现状述评概括性特别好，主要的概念一目了然：效度理论，效度验证模式和三项考试的研究及存在的不足。把前人的研究清晰地进行了梳理，也提出了前人研究的不足及仍需进行的研究。这部分多读几遍，可以学习写综述。本课题的研究内容这一块，今天刚好看到了效度概念，语言测试词典上关于效度的英文术语我看了觉得不太明白，但是在辜老师的申报书里通过效度后面的几个问题能够很快明白这几个效度概念的含义，特别是认知效度和效标关联效度。研究思路和方法这个图形给我的印象特别深刻，这种呈现出自己研究过程的方式特别好。以前也看过别人的申请书里有路径图，但是有的看起来很复杂。这里的过程清楚，内容一目了然。最后，具体方法这里有两个方法比较特别，一种是有声思维，还有一个是眼动实验。这两个方法做的难度是不是会很高？

感悟：让我印象特别深刻的是前期的相关研究，成果丰硕。好的选题不是一朝一夕就能想出来的，必须靠前期扎扎实实的阅读和学习，一步一步研究，慢慢积累而来。我之前看过辜老师介绍过最终版的申报书的出炉经历：个人撰写、个人修改、团队修改、国内外专家修改，选题的文字修改也是经历了几个回合，申报书一起改了好像有十几稿。一份高质量的申报书只有经过反复打磨才能出来。认真做一件有价值的事，反复做一件有价值的事，总有一天会有回报。

参考作答 2

摘录自辜老师的申报书：

课题国内外研究现状述评："基于证据的效度验证框架"（Weir 2005）从社会认知视角出发，涵盖五个方面的效验证据：基于理论的效度、环境效度、评分效度、效标关联效度和后果效度，可操作性较强，并在剑桥主体证书考试（KET、PET、FCE、CAE、CPE）的效度对比研究中得到丰富和完善，将基于理论的效度更名为认知效度，受试特征也成为效验证据很重要的方面（Shaw & Weir 2007；Khalifa & Weir 2009；Taylor2011；Geranpayeh & Taylor 2013）。

课题研究的主要内容：

本课题拟从 Weir（2005）"基于证据的效度验证框架"出发，从六个方面对大学英语四六级、雅思、托福进行较全面深入的考试效度对比研究。具体内容和研究问题如下。

受试特征：三项考试涉及受试的哪些生理、心理和体验特征？

环境效度：三项考试测试任务的环境和操作对所有受试是否公平？

认知效度：受试完成三项考试测试任务的认知过程和交互活动是否真实？

评分效度：三项考试的评分及考试分数在多大程度上是可靠的？

后果效度：三项考试对受试的心理状态和学习过程产生了什么影响？

效标关联效度：三项考试的分数是否一致性较高？是否可以进行等值？

这些具体内容和研究问题最终指向并回答一个总的问题：三项考试的效度有何异同？

基本观点：

尽管四六级、雅思、托福这三项考试的目的、性质、构念、分数解释和结果使用等诸多方面存在不同，但三项考试都是以英语为外语或二语的大规模、高风险语言考试，受试将接受或正在接受高等教育，三项考试应该具有可比性，三者的效度应该既有较大的相似性，也存在一定的差异。而实际情况是否如此，有待进行全面深入的实证研究。

收获：

科研项目选题源于教学实践，优秀的科研项目需要不断精益求精。看了老师的国家社科课题申请书，内心十分震撼。这份表格里的文献综述看似简短，句子短小精悍，但是精练的后面是深度而广泛的学术研读、提炼和深思。每一个 technical term 用词都非常精准、恰当，从效度的定义到它的验证模式、验证框架，不仅论述全面，而且高度提炼的观点表述非常连贯和自然。成功，真的源于真实、自然。

参考作答 3

自 20 世纪 60 年代以来，效度理论取得了从"分类效度观"到"整体效度观"的重大发展。分类效度观（Lado, 1961）认为效度可分为效标关联效度、内容效度、构念效度。整体效度观给出了具有突破意义的效度定义，即"对经验证据和理论依据在多大程度上支持分数的解释与使用进行的综合评价就是效度"（Messick, 1989:13）

"基于证据的效度验证框架"（Weir, 2005）从社会认知视角出发，涵盖五个方面的效验证据：基于理论的效度、环境效度、评分效度、效标关联效度和后果效度。

受试特征：三项考试涉及受试的哪些生理、心理和体验特征？

环境效度：三项考试测试任务的环境和操作对所有受试是否公平？

认知效度：受试完成三项考试测试任务的认知过程和交互活动是否真实？

评分效度：三项考试的评分及考试分数在多大程度上是可靠的？

后果效度：三项考试对受试的心理状态和学习过程产生了什么影响？

效标关联效度：三项考试的分数是否一致性较高？是否可以进行等值？

理解和收获：

从书上的图表来看，主要是先从受试开始，受试要完成任务，就要在一定的环境下进行，环境效度就是其中一个影响因素；接着，受试想要完成任务就需要有一定的认知过程与交互活动，就涉及认知效度；在受试完成任务之后，会对其表现进行评分，这涉及评分效度；结果出来之后，就涉及如何解释这个分数，这个分数会有些什么影响，也就是由这个分数延伸出来的效标关联效度以及后果效度；最后由构念效度对这些进行总体的控制来保证其能够进行有效的测试。

举个例子，去完成一个任务，分外在和内在的影响因素，外在的就是环境效度，内在的就是认知效度；完成任务之后，会对表现进行评分，就有了评分效度；之后由分数引发的对个人和社会产生的影响，就有了效标关联效度和后果效度；最后由构念效度统一把控。

7. 你赞同大规模测试的四点优势吗（p.90）？请谈谈你校或你本人是如何使用我国相关的大规模语言测试结果／数据的？

参考作答 1

赞同。本人多次担任英语专业基础阶段的综合英语课程的教学任务，每年都会关注学生的英语专业四级考试结果。如果自己教过的学生当年参加了专四考试，就要总结哪些方面的教学做得好，哪些做得不好，为下一批学生的教学吸取经验和教训。如果自己教的学生当年未参加专四考试，也会关注考试结果，了解一下学生各项得分的情况，作为自己教学的参考信息，也提醒学生应该加强哪一方面的学习。以上做法就是利用大规模语言测试结果作为 evidence of learning 来衡量自己的教学效果，也利用考试结果作为 evidence for learning，作为加强某方面教学的依据。

参考作答 2

赞同。大型考试确实有其无可比拟的优势，包括其基于标准对考试分数的解释，构念为基础（考查真实世界所需能力），运用了强有力的测量模型，同时也可以对个人不同方面的语言能力进行报告（如雅思小分）。

8. 请问你是否有认真完整地阅读过相关的教学大纲（如高中的新课标、大学英语课程标准、英语专业本科教学质量国家标准等）？如果没有，请查找阅读，并谈谈你阅读后的收获。

参考作答 1

阅读过 2020 年《普通高中英语课程标准》。

收获：《普通高中英语课程标准》的修订体现了思想性和时代性，不仅承载和体现了国家意志，也是多年来普通高中课程改革的成果。新课标的修订全面且深入，明确了普通高中英语教育的定位，并提出了提升学生综合素质和发展核心素养的要求，指引性地描绘出教育的本质和方向。除了明确提出四项核心素养，英语新课标还从课程结构、课程内容、学业质量和实施建议等方面进行改革，不仅指明了教育的方向，还规划出了具体的实施路径和评价标准，能够更好地帮助职前和在职教师理解英语新课标，并将其运用到教育教学实践中。

参考作答 2

阅读过《商务英语专业本科教学质量国家标准》。

收获：对商务英语专业的学生的人才培养目标、培养规格、培养能力、课程框架、教学与评价等有大致了解。我觉得教学大纲是课程开展的基础，阅读教学大纲可以全面地了解课程要求，了解教学目标，了解知识要求以及学生的能力要求等，对我们的教学会有很好的启示和指导作用。

9. 请问你是否认真完整地阅读过我国的大规模英语测试（如高考英语、大学英语四六级考试、英语专业四八级考试、全国硕士研究生入学英语考试等）的考试大纲？如果没有，请查找阅读，并谈谈你阅读后的收获。

参考作答 1

没有读过考试大纲。

收获：考试大纲把要求写得非常明确。就听力而言，大学英语四六级的考试大纲是要求四级听懂语速较慢的短篇英语广播、报道、对话等；而六级则需要听懂语速中等的报道、讲话以及学术讲座等。每分钟的语速四六级之间相差20词。根据这些要求，我们在准备考试的时候不一定非要去刷题，而是可以在平时多听新闻广播，语速可以从慢到快，锻炼听力。按照考试大纲要求的更高一级去备考应该就没有大问题。

参考作答 2

由于参加过类似的大规模考试，特别是影响比较大的专四、专八考试等，对于其考试大纲是认真研读过的，因为需要按照大纲进行相关的备考。整体来说，大纲要求能够测试考生相关的水平，并且也比较与时俱进（如专四2016年进行了改革）。但是对比之前的研读和这次的阅读，我还是觉得大纲要求中的某些描述语比较模糊，而且不是特别实际。例如专八听力要求"能够听懂真实交际场合的各种英语会话和讲话"，这个要求很难达到，而且没有相关的限定，学生无从下手准备。

10. 请查阅我国大规模语言测试分数解释 / 报道的权威性文献和我国大规模语言测试发展历程的权威性文献，在群里分享并谈谈你的阅读收获。

参考作答

（1）金艳，杨惠中. 走中国特色的语言测试道路：大学英语四、六级考试三十年的启示 [J]. 外语界，2018(2)：29-39.

收获：本文回顾四、六级考试三十年来的改革和发展历程，阐述其对大学英语教学发展的作用，并结合语言测试的效度理论，探索我国语言测试进一步改革和发展的方向。文章指出，为打造具有中国特色的考试项目，必须重视我国外语教育的国情，深入思考语言测试的社会学问题，坚持走具有中国特色的语言测试道路，使我国的品牌考试更加稳健发展，并在不远的将来走出国门，面向世界。我个人认为这是从中国与世界的角度来探讨大学英语四、六级考试。

（2）王海啸.从系统的角度看大学英语四、六级考试改革——"大学英语四、六级考试改革社会调查课题"调研报告 [J].中国外语，2008(4)：4-12.

收获：从系统的角度看，大学英语考试是大学英语教学这个系统的一部分，而大学英语教学和高等教育的一部分，高等教育则是社会的一部分。社会、高等教育和大学英语教学即成为大学英语考试的上层系统。另外，大学英语考试本身也包括命题、施考、阅卷、发布成绩等不同环节。这些不同环节即构成大学英语教学考试的下层系统。改革大学英语教学既要从考试的上层系统入手，也要从考试的下层系统入手。本文依据一项大规模问卷调查的结果，探讨大学英语考试与其上、下层系统的关系，对大学英语考试改革提出了一些建设性意见。个人认为这是从整个社会教育的角度来探讨大学英语四、六级考试的。

（3）金艳，郭杰克.大学英语四、六级考试非面试型口语考试效度研究 [J].外语界，2002(5)：72-79.

收获：为适应不断扩大的四、六级口语考试规模，也为了给没有条件实施CET-SET 地区的广大考生提供一个更具现实可操作性的口语能力测量手段，四、六级考试委员会开发了以录音方式进行的 CET-SOPT 。本研究初步论证了 CET-SOPT 与 CET-SET 的可比性，也证明了 CET-SOPT 的效度、信度和较强的可操作性。但作为间接性口语能力测试，CET-SOPT 不可避免地具有缺乏真实口语交际中的交互性这一缺陷。这是从大学英语四、六级考试自身改革的角度进行的探讨。

总结：大学英语四、六级考试经历了多次改革，从无到有，从有到分（这里主要指口语考试），从单一英语考试到对整个教育体制的影响，甚至从国内到走出国门，逐步逐层在深化，希望这也是我们这一代英语教育者能够有所贡献的地方。

11. 请查看国内大规模语言测试的官网，并对比国外的大规模语言测试的官网（如雅思、托福考试的官网），对比其异同。

参考作答 1

相同点：都有题型分布介绍以及分数解释；都公布考试时间。

不同点：在官网上，雅思有样题；四六级和托福没有样题；四六级有考试大纲，雅思托福没有；国外的大规模语言测试网站还为学生提供了一些备考方案和备考途径等，同时也列举出了一些经常遇到的问题，并做出了回答，这一点相对于国内的考试来说是较为完善的。

参考作答 2

相同点：之前查找过相关的样题，两者相似的是对于大纲和考试题型、考试时间、考试安排、分数解读都有相应的解释。

不同点：相较而言，雅思和托福给出了更多相关的资料参考，类似于真题视频、音频等，同时在官网介绍了一些 research projects，what the IELT take you 的相关信息，我想应该是为了解释考试用的。因为托福和雅思是面向全球的考试，专门设计了中国网站，而四六级由于是面向国内的考试，只有一个官网。

第七章　面向学习的课堂评价
Chapter 7　Learning-oriented assessment in the classroom

章节目录

1. 思维导图呈现本章目录

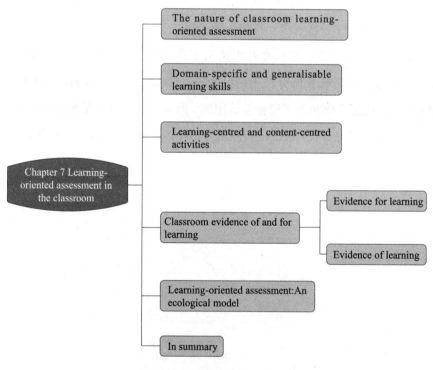

图 7.1　第七章思维导图目录

2. 表格呈现本章目录

表 7.1 第七章表格目录

7 Learning–oriented assessment in the classroom	第七章 面向学习的课堂评价
THE NATURE OF CLASSROOM LEARNING-ORIENTED ASSESSMENT	7.1 面向学习的课堂评价的本质
DOMAIN-SPECIFIC AND GENERALISABLE LEARNING SKILLS	7.2 特定领域和通用学习技能
LEARNING-CENTRED AND CONTENT-CENTRED ACTIVITIES	7.3 以学习为中心和以内容为中心的活动
CLASSROOM EVIDENCE OF AND FOR LEARNING Evidence for learning Evidence of learning	7.4 以评测学和以评促学课堂 7.4.1 以评促学 7.4.2 以评测学
LEARNING-ORIENTED ASSESSMENT: AN ECOLOGICAL MODEL	7.5 面向学习的测评：一种生态模式
IN SUMMARY	7.6 小结

补充思考题及参考作答

1. **请翻译杜威名句（Give the pupils something to do, not something to learn and the doing is of such a nature as to demand thinking; learning naturally results.），并谈谈你对该名句的理解。**

参考作答 1

　　翻译：教师应该让学生有任务可做，而不是一味学习，这种做任务的本质是促使学生动脑思考，这个时候学习就自然地发生了。

　　Dewey expressed the idea of "learning by doing" in this quote. He argued that priority should be given to task-doing in a classroom, instead of content-learning. This reminds me of the debate addressed in Section 7.3 around learning-centered activities and content-centered activities. Although learning-centered activities are beneficial for promoting communicative skills, it cannot be ignored that content-centered teaching and learning provide the ground for students to effectively accomplish the tasks. Without conscious learning of the target knowledge, students might have no clues of what they can or should do for the task. Therefore, I would rather support Jones and Saville's argument that learning and doing are complementary to each other.

参考作答 2

翻译：给学生实际做的机会，而不仅仅是学习。这种做的过程其本质是需要思考的，在这样的情况下，学习会自然发生。

理解：这句名言和老师经常强调的"在做中学"（learning by doing）有异曲同工之妙。社会建构主义强调学习需要通过"交互"（interaction）产生，是一种社会过程，在实际做的过程中才知道自己做得对不对、好不好，下一步应该怎样推动。结合本章中的 cycle of assessment 来看，不仅仅是让学生做来激发思考，更要在学生做后给出评价和反馈，这样促进学习的效果会更好。

2. LOA 课堂的本质是什么？

参考作答 1

LOA 课堂的本质是：在课堂活动中，师生、生生之间进行积极而有意义的交互。这种交互过程中，测评四要素：表现、观察、解释、反馈循环反复参与其中，从而使学习产生（produces learning），学生的个性得以发展。

参考作答 2

书上几处提到了 LOA 课堂的本质，这里借用专著第七章开头第 93 页，以及结尾第 104-105 页的内容回答这个问题。

专著第 93 页有这样一段话：This chapter presents two major concerns of the learning-oriented classroom: to generate interactions which lead to learning, and to capture evidence of interaction, in ways that maximize the impact of further learning. 我的理解是：这一章聚焦 LOA 课堂中的两个重点：第一是以促学为目标的互动，第二是捕获互动的证据，目的是最大化对未来学习的影响。

专著第 104-105 页列举了 LOA 课堂的一些特征：1）课堂互动的本质是要促成"表现—观察—解释—反馈"这样一个循环；2）学生要能够管理自己的学习，老师起到辅助的作用；3）互动中要搭建支架以及要有合适的课堂任务；4）学生使用语言要注重语言意义的表达，课堂活动也应适量注重语言形式；5）互动要真实，以此让学生产生内在学习动机；6）语言能力的本质是技能，而语言技能的产生既要依赖以学习为中心的课堂活动，也要依赖以语言本身为中心的课堂活动；7）学习即个人成长的过程，这包括学会如何学习的技巧；8）课程目标链接两个层面的评估手段，目的是促学。

总的来说，LOA 课堂的本质应该包括几个重点：1）要有以促学为目标的互动，互动要促成"表现—观察—解释—反馈"这样一个循环；2）互动中要搭建支架以及互动中的任务要合适；3）互动要真实，以此激发内在学习动力；4）学生在互动中既注重意义的传达，也参与聚焦语言形式的课堂活动；5）学生管理自己的学习，老师辅助；6）学习的目的不仅是高阶语言技能的产生，还应包括学会如何学习。

参考作答 3

要了解课堂中 LOA 的本质，首先要了解如果课堂互动促进学习，那么为什么能够促进以及它是如何促进学习的。

首先，课堂互动需要依托学习活动，学习活动的开展需要以学习任务为中心，学习任务的设定需要教师创设学习环境，学生需要在学习过程中培养自主学习的技能。同时教师要对这种学习互动进行观察，解释并能够做出反馈，从而实现评估循环（performance—observation—interpretation—feedback），进而促进学习。这就是 LOA 倡导的系统性。

其次，LOA 在课堂中学生的学习技能包括特定领域的学习技能和可泛化 / 迁移的学习技能（domain-specific and generalizable learning skills），学习活动包括以学习为中心的活动和以内容为中心的（leaning-centered and content-centered）活动。

再次，LOA 模式中的课堂以评测学（evidence of learning）以及以评促学（evidence for learning）是在评估循环的过程中获取的，是一种基于过程的证据。学习证据中的大规模测评和课堂评价证据互补，以评促学需要依据以学习为中心的活动和以内容为中心的活动共同作用。

最后，LOA 是一种系统的生态模型。整个评估过程是一个评估循环，在过程中进行评估，外部评估与课堂评价互补，外部证据与内部证据互补，在此过程中提升语言技能，实现个人发展，进而形成社会建构主义的学习模式。

3. 请谈谈你对 Figure 7.1（p.98）的解读。

参考作答 1

The figure consists of two circles: an inner circle of classroom-based assessment and an outer circle of external curriculum and assessment. The inner circle represents the assessment circle of performance-observation-interpretation-feedback (p.94), which refers to the activities in the classroom on meaningful interaction based on the given syllabus. The outer circle represents the curriculum and assessment imposed on the classroom. This involves the frame of reference, which describes different language levels; the learning objectives, which draw on the reference's description; the syllabus, which reflects the learning objectives; the external exam, which assesses learning; and the record of achievement, which includes both formative and summative assessment results, provides sources for the interpretation of the students' performance against the frame of reference and informs the construction of future learning objectives and syllabus.

参考作答 2

Figure7.1 presents both macro and micro cycles of an LOA. The macro cycle is composed of learning objectives (goals of learning) → external exam (to check whether the goals are achieved or not) → record of achievement (the evidence of and for learning) → interpretation (to align students proficiency with CEFR levels) → iterated learning objective (to modify or improve the original learning objectives based on advanced students' proficiency). The micro cycle is task-based and comprises the flows of task → language activity → teacher observation → interpretation → decision making → feedback or modify learning objectives → iterated task.

参考作答 3

这个图表呈现的是面向学习的测评的课堂教学模型。图左的环形是微观层面的课堂教学：围绕以任务为形式的 LOA 活动开展，其步骤包含教师发布任务，学生在教师的指导下采取互动方式完成任务，教师观察学生完成任务的过程并进行解读，将解读的结果进行记录。这些记录一方面可以指导教师进行决策、提供反馈和改变教学目标。以上这些，最后都回到下一个任务中，这个新的任务可以达到检测先前知识的作用。另一方面，这些记录也以结构化的形式出现，作为学生的成绩记录。图表外围呈现的是宏观层面的面向学习的测评：教学目标更加具体，包含了高层次的学习能力。这一目标一方面指导 LOA 课堂教学的教学大纲，进入到微观层面的课堂教学；另一方面这一目标指导外部测试，测试结果又可作为学生成绩的记录。这样，学生的成绩记录就包含了课堂教学的结构化记录和外部测试的成绩。成绩记录一方面作为形成性监控指导课堂教学目标的制定，另一方面用参考框架（如 CEFR）来解释，指导宏观教学目标的制定。

4. 请重读 7.6 In summary (pp.104–105) 面向学习的课堂特征，对照这些特征反思我们自己的教学实践，看有哪些方面需要改进？

参考作答 1

There are a few things I could draw on during teaching design. Firstly, content teaching, tests and comments are not the only components of a language class; assessment cycle of performance, observation, evaluation, and feedback should be included. Secondly, scaffolding can be a powerful tool that supports students learning. How teachers construct their words of instruction is an important issue. Thirdly, task design is crucial in a language class. It would be helpful to bear in mind the author's definition of task: the purposeful use of language to communicate personally significant meanings (p.41).

参考作答 2

改进之处：

（1）没有有意识地运用学习循环，以后要增强这种意识。

（2）关于教师和学生的角色，教师作为互动的 facilitator 要知道需要做什么、怎么做才能帮助学生实现自主学习，而不是被迫学习，至少在课堂要注意培养学生自主学习的习惯，以便学生逐渐形成习惯。

（3）学习互动的支撑和活动的设计，以前没有特殊关注过。

（4）语言使用欠缺很多，尤其是最近实行网络教学，基本是用汉语与学生沟通（我的学生虽然是本科生，但是他们是艺体类学生，英语基础较弱）。

（5）注意活动设计要支持学生的学习。

（6）学习任务设置需要更清晰有效。

（7）学习活动的时间分配需要更合理。

（8）个人发展中的可泛化／可迁移技能培养。

（9）与外部大规模测评的结合几乎没有。不同专业的学生对英语要求不一样，有的专业甚至没有任何要求，只要完成英语课程，分数及格及以上就可以，所以很少考虑这个方面。

参考作答 3

结合本章 In summary，我认为我的教学实践有以下方面需要改进：

（1）LOA 课堂的评价是一个环形，包含学生的表现、教师的观察、评估和反馈。我感觉自己在教学过程中评估和反馈给得不够及时或者给出了反馈后，没有再继续跟进，既没有去了解反馈是否对学生产生了影响，也没有进一步对教学活动进行改进。

（2）也许是由于第一个需要改进的问题，即给出了反馈后没有继续跟进每个学生的学习进程，因此我并没有掌握每个学生是否得到了恰当的支持。

（3）LOA 要求课程目标和大规模测试相关联，我觉得我在教学中是把这两种测评看成了两个独立个体，没有想过如何去结合这两种测评。

参考作答 4

改进之处：

第一点，在反馈方面，更多是课后作业的书面反馈，或是偶尔的面对面口头反馈。课堂上反馈明显不足。

第二点，作为老师，难点在于如何让所有学生都具有管理自己学习的能力。

第三点，如何让每一个学生都得到充足的支持？

第四点，让所有学生都积极参与活动过程是个考验。

第五点，learning-centred 以及 content-centered work 的分配还要多加考虑。

5. 请分享你或者你的老师的课堂测评实践，并结合 Figure 7.1 对这些实践进行自评。

参考作答 1

我个人课堂的测评实践目标不那么清晰，评估循环有时候也没有注意到，活动和任务的设计也没有考虑评估，反馈仅仅注意分数的差异没有深究原因，更没有考虑与外部测试的互补。教学大纲只是上课必备的材料，没有真正地指导教学。课堂上，对学生的表现记录，仅仅关注参与的次数，对学生课堂的进步过程，没有记录的习惯，缺乏持续的关注。

参考作答 2

现阶段课程中，老师的课堂测评实践主要是基于目标让我们完成相应的任务，并在课堂上进行展示，老师观察并给出相关的反馈和评价。我觉得按照 "performance—observation—interpretation—feedback" 的这个测评循环来说，我们可以展示自己，也能得到老师相应的反馈和点评。但是我觉得最缺乏的是对相关表现的解读，标准是什么呢？ LOA 模型中解读的部分是结合了 CEFR，这是比较权威的标准，但是在我们的课堂上这种评价标准还是比较模糊的。同时在 record of achievement 那一部分，也不太清楚，因为老师很少公布这类记录。

第八章 大规模测评和课堂评价的对接
Chapter 8 Aligning large-scale and classroom assessment

章节目录

1. 思维导图呈现本章目录

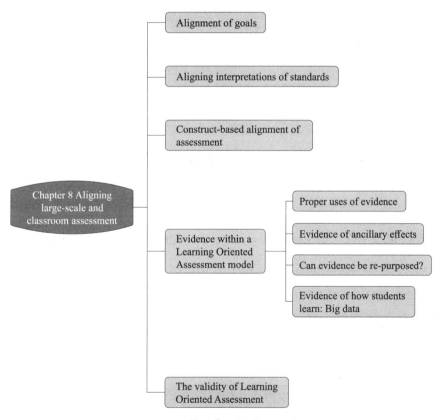

图 8.1 第八章思维导图目录

2. 表格呈现本章目录

表 8.1　第八章表格目录

8 Aligning large–scale and classroom assessment	第八章 大规模测评和课堂评价的对接
ALIGNMENT OF GOALS	8.1 目标对接
ALIGNING INTERPRETATIONS OF STANDARDS	8.2 对接标准解释
CONSTRUCT-BASED ALIGNMENT OF ASSESSMENT	8.3 基于构念的测评对接
EVIDENCE WITHIN A LEARNING ORIENTED ASSESSMENT MODEL Proper uses of evidence Evidence of ancillary effects Can evidence be re-purposed? Evidence of how students learn: Big data	8.4 面向学习的测评模型中的证据 8.4.1 证据的恰当使用 8.4.2 附加效应的证据 8.4.3 证据可以被重新利用吗？ 8.4.4 学生如何学习的证据：大数据
THE VALIDITY OF LEARNING ORIENTED ASSESSMENT	8.5 面向学习的测评效度

补充思考题及参考作答

1. 翻译杜威名句（The two limits of every unit of thinking are a perplexed, troubled, or confused situation at the beginning, and a cleared up, unified, resolved situation at the close.）。结合本章内容，谈谈你对此名句的理解。

参考作答 1

翻译：每段思维都有两个节点，最初的迷茫、困惑、混乱和最终的清晰、明了、统一。

理解：我个人想用"段"这个词来表述"unit"的含义，这个"段"可能是一件事情持续的时间，可能是一段体验持续的时间，也可能是一个活动持续的时间，也可能就是一个思想持续的时间，这个时间没有长短的限制。总之一段是一个完整的始终，也体现出一个过程，这个过程可长可短。我认为该句揭示出了思维所经历的过程以及思考者的心理状态。本章标题是"大规模测评和课堂评价的对接"，最初感觉很模糊，都结合了什么内容，怎么结合，为什么要这样结合？其实作者最后给了我们答案就是建构一个综合模式，即 LOA 模式，与杜威的名句体现出来的思想一致。

参考作答 2

翻译：思考的两个极限是从最初的困惑、混乱和糊涂到最终的明白、整合和坚定。

理解：本章主要内容是将大规模测试和课堂评价结合起来建立一个综合模式，帮助读者理解外部测试和课堂评价的证据，同时两方面的评价要聚焦于共同的标准和目标。相关的测试和评价的证据，或者说整个学习过程，对我们来说都是比较混乱、难以理解的，在建立了相关的框架和综合评价后，以及在如何解读相关证据的过程中，会像杜威名言后半句一样，感到清晰、统一，之前的困惑也能得到解决。

参考作答 3

翻译：每个思考单位都有两个极限，即最初的迷惘、困惑、不解和最后的明朗、统一、问题得到解决。

理解：且把"思考"看作"LOA 如何促学"，那么考虑这个问题时也有两个极限，即"最初的迷惘"或许可以是"不知怎样综合大规模测评以及课堂评价"，"最后的统一"或许可以是"大规模测评和课堂评价最终形成互补"，那么这句话实际上是在描述这一个过程，恰好第八章也是在谈论这个主题。

2. 请再拟一遍本章的目录，从本章论述的五个方面反思与自评你的教、学、测、评实践。

参考作答 1

（1）目录

8.1 Alignment of goals

Alignment of goals is required that what is taught is what is tested, and that both serve purposes deemed to be of value to society.

8.2 Aligning interpretations of standards

It is critical that all levels of assessment understand performance standards in the same way.

8.3 Construct-based alignment of assessment

Figure 8.1 illustrates the roles performed within each of the (four) worlds and the factors which impact on learning. It is not specifically a model of language learning. ... if we accept that there should be coherence between school subjects and skills valued in society, language should be taught as a useful skill, and consequently there is a solid framework in teaching that assessment in teaching and assessment practice can be built on.

8.4 Evidence within a Learning Oriented Assessment model

Two fundamental purposes of assessment: to describe and report outcomes of learning (better measurement), and to bring about further learning—evidence of and for learning (better learning)

Validity: the assurances that the evidence which an assessment furnishes is fit for the purposed it claims to serve.

The assessment cycle must be implemented in all contexts with sufficient care that the evidence provide is credible.

8.4.1 Proper use of evidence

Data on students' performance should be used in the first instance to assist teachers to judge their own effectiveness (relative to local or national benchmarks), although the model also permits other key stakeholders (principals, ministries, parents, students) to share this evidence.

8.4.2 Evidence of ancillary effects

It is to approach ancillary skills (personal development) indirectly through measuring the primary learning outcomes (communicative language ability).

8.4.3 Can evidence be re-purposed?

It is quite unreasonable to expect that a measure constructed from the results of lower-level observations should correlate highly with students' demonstration of higher-order communicative skills.

8.4.4 Evidence of how students learn: Big data

Evidence for learning based on big data is likely to become an increasingly significant field in the coming years.

8.5 The validity of Learning Oriented Assessment

It reviews the issues that need to be addressed in any implementation, and evidence of validity which might be provided.

（2）自评

我个人教学的实践中缺少清晰的测评目标和测评标准，测评的设计对于测评实践和相应证据的获取及解释缺乏科学性指导，因此，测评结果很难作为科学的学习证据或者促学证据，也无法达到促学的效果。教学的实践以这次的导读任务为例，对我个人来讲，这次学习目标清晰，标准统一，效果明显：此次导读从任务入手，通过不同的活动（自读和导读），教师的观察、指导和反馈等完成体现评估循环，也无一不在促进我们的学习。

重新理出来的目录与之前的目录概述有很多差异，我个人认为这次的目录更清晰，重点更突出，可能是因为再看一遍文章内容，对文章内容有了更深刻的了解。

参考作答2

自评

在我的教学实践中，教学目标是参考教学大纲中的要求，结合章节重难点，以及学生情感目标来写的，但是测试的时候我用的是学校统一要求的试卷。实话实说，我的教案中所写的目标和学生考试试卷脱节，唯一的结合点就是考点，这样做能不能发挥以评促学的作用呢？应该说作用是很小的，因为课堂的重点就是考点，很少有精力去拓展别的内容。

3. 请用Green(2012)建议的方法(p.109)分析《中国英语能力等级量表》7级中的能做描述语，并分享你的发现。

参考作答1

（1）《中国英语能力等级量表》7级

Can understand language materials on a range of topics, including those related to his/her field of specialization; can accurately identify the theme and key points of the material, objectively assess and comment on its content, and understand its deeper meaning.

Can engage in in-depth discussion and exchange with others on a range of related academic and social topics; can effectively describe, clarify, explain, justify, and comment on such matters and express him/herself clearly, appropriately, smoothly, and in a conventional manner.

（2）描述语

Activity: Can understand; can identify; can assess and comment; can engage; can describe, clarify, explain, justify, comment and express.

Topic: language materials related to his/her field of specialization, the theme and key points of the materials, a range of academic and social topics.

Input text: language materials on a range of topics.

Qualities: accurately, objectively, deeper, in-depth, effectively, clearly, appropriately, smoothly.

Restrictions: with others, in a conventional manner.

（3）发现

能够利用该框架把 CSE7 级中能做描述语归入相应的主题。利用这个框架可以加深对 CSE 各级别的能做描述语进行分析，以便更好地理解描述语的内容。

参考作答 2

（1）描述语

Activity: 能理解多种话题的语言材料，能就多种相关学术和社会话题进行深入交流和讨论；

Theme/Topic: 多种话题，包括自己所学专业领域；

Input text: 多种话题的语言材料，包括自己所学专业领域的学术性材料；

Output text: 多种相关学术和社会话题进行深入交流和讨论；

Qualities: 准确把握主旨和要义，客观审视、评析材料的内容，理解深层含义；有效地进行描述、说明、解释、论证和评析；

Restrictions: 表达规范、清晰、得体、顺畅。

（2）发现

能够利用该框架把 CSE7 级中能做描述语归入相应的主题。能利用这个框架深入分析 CSE 各级别的能做描述语，更深入地理解描述语的内容，自身在进行教学 / 学习实践的时候，对应进行自评和他评。

4. 请用 Figure 8.1 Four worlds of learning revisited（p.112）作为参考框架，评价你的教学实践。

参考作答 1

看到这个题目浮现在脑子里的就是"天上地下"这四个字，我的教学跟这个图差别太大。

首先我的课堂教学不是以 task 为中心的，或者说我用的 task 至少不是 Van

den Branden 定义的那一种 task；其次四个世界"个人—教育—社会—测评"在我的教学里面好像很少情况下是紧密相连的。我的学生（中学生）几乎只在英语课上说英语，到社会上在大街上看到一些欧美商品品牌的时候，好像也不知道如何用英语技能，所以跟社会联系比较松散；学生跟测评这一块接触频繁，因为每一周都有英语考试；说起学习目标的话，除了我会在课前和课中介绍，好像也没有看到学生在哪里找教学目标看；最后，教育局（算教育界，其实也和测评有关）跟学生联系紧密，但是对达成课程目标的要求方面好像比关注学生测试结果方面要少得多，反过来看测评对于学生个人的影响（这个是我根据我学生的表现反推的），测评有时候会起到激励的作用（比如英语好的学生会一直在学英语上面很用心），有时只会给学生徒增压力（比如英语考不好的学生干脆放弃学习，上课专门睡觉）。总的来说，这个图和我的教学实践就像是"天上地下"。

但是在接下来的教学实践中，可以尝试让学生在生活中去发现英语，并拍照带到课堂来，比如家里吃的、穿的、用的、玩的……但我们几乎没有让学生意识到英语与我们每天的日常紧密相关。再让他们做一个实践项目：街拍公共场所的英语，也会发现很多。我们几乎所有的学科都存在书本教学与实际生活脱节的情况。如果我们再去看中小学课标，非常强调与生活实践的关联，老师们需要认真学习课标，在教学中去实践"学以致用"的理念。

参考作答 2

说起个人的教学实践，感觉很惭愧，从教时间在这里显得几乎没有什么意义和价值。我的教学实践兼顾了这四个世界，但是每一个部分都存在着问题，四个世界没有通过评估联系起来；任务作为教学活动的中心缺少科学合理的设计；互动、评估和反馈也没有起到应有的作用，因此评估的过程没有呈现该有的评估循环；以评测学和以评促学的实现程度也有待探讨，而形成性评估和终结性评估的内容、过程和成绩也需要继续斟酌。

5. 请问你在教学实践中都用了哪些方法，收集了哪些方面的测评数据 / 证据？请自评这些方法和数据的有效性。

参考作答 1

　　首先建立相关的学习档案，例如写周记、读书笔记、回顾。我觉得这个办法是比较有效的（虽然执行起来有点痛苦），能够对我日常学习的过程、轨迹、内容以及成就都有所记录；授课教师、导师、同辈的反馈也很有效，能够一针见血地指出我的不足，并且很多时候可以给我一些改进的建议；还有一个办法是参加相关的大规模考试，以该次考试的分数来检验自己那一段时间的学习状况，这个办法也挺好的。但是，缺点是这个办法的结果也许不能一概而论，因为分数不一定能够完全反映一个人的能力，会有很多影响因素，比如考试本身难度等。

参考作答 2

　　在我的教学实践中，测评数据的来源有：学生的课堂表现，练习和作业中出现的错误，考试中的答题数据，如区分度和难度、及格率、优秀率等。主要方法是观察法、比较法。

　　从了解学生的角度看，有效性还是不错的。教学有效性方面，还会有多种因素的制约。

6. 请从你的视角尝试回答 8.5 小节中的六个效度问题（pp.118–120）。

参考作答

　　1) What are the quality criteria? How can reliability and validity be reconceptualized within a socio-cultural framework?

　　To ensure the quality criteria, large-scale assessment and classroom assessment are introduced as the quantitative and qualitative dimension to measure the higher-order skills and lower-level achievements of the learners. Tasks are placed at the center of the learning activity, followed by interaction, observation and feedback in the assessment cycle. Tasks are also the center of the four worlds, and it is the assessment world that brings the other three worlds together.

Evidence of learning and for learning in large-scale assessment and classroom assessment is provided to achieve high-level of reliability without the compromising on validity.

2) What are the characteristics of the assessment tasks that provide a context for learning? What is the evidence for these bringing about change in learning?

Assessment tasks that provide a context for learning are those that can promote meaningful and purposeful interaction from the students.

The evidence of change in learning can be demonstrated from the students' performance in large-scale assessment and classroom assessment.

3) What is the nature of teacher/student feedback and reflection that influences the effort towards and outcome of further learning?

To promote further learning is one of the goals of assessment. In the classroom, it is the roles of the teachers and the students that matter. The teachers should have a positive view about their roles and duties concerning teaching, assessment and reporting. And the students should overcome any prior negative learning experience and develop a positive disposition to learning.

4) What defines the role(s) and responsibilities of "assessor"? How do teachers and students interpret their roles? What impacts on their decision-making?

The roles or responsibilities of "assessor" are to make sure the authentic assessment of the learners' performance, report the record of their achievement and interpret the learning outcomes to promote learning.

The assessors can be external assessment organizations, the school or even the teachers themselves, and the students themselves. Their roles or responsibilities will have a positive or negative impact on learning. So, the assessment should go with great validity and reliability based on big data. The use of the evidence should have no impact on their purpose of assessment.

7. Chapters 2 & 8 没有 In Summary，为什么？

参考作答 1

第 2 章是对于 LOA 的理论基础的文献综述，本身就是总结性的章节，所以不需要再额外写一个总结；第 8 章是基于第 6、7 章提出的一个综合模式，本身也具有总结性，所以也不需要额外的总结部分。

参考作答 2

对比这两章之后，个人觉得两章的共同特性就是最后一部分都是对本章前面部分的总结或者根据前面内容得出来的结论，其实也带有总结性的特征，因此如果再额外加入总结，有些画蛇添足。此外，以本书作者惜墨如金、启人深思的写作风格，最后一部分不再额外进行总结，也在情理之中。如果两章都加上 In Summary，也未尝不可，但是作者还是选择由读者来进行思考，可能更有意义。

参考作答 3

可能的一个原因是写作风格未统一；另外一个原因也许是作者其实对于主题进行了比较细致的回答，例如第 8 章，引入，提出 LOA 模型，相关证据和效度验证都有论证，但作者也提到目前的困难（实施要求高、改变相关认知的必要性），不需要再进行总结。

第九章 实施面向学习的测评
Chapter 9 Implementing Learning Oriented Assessment

章节目录

1. 思维导图呈现本章目录

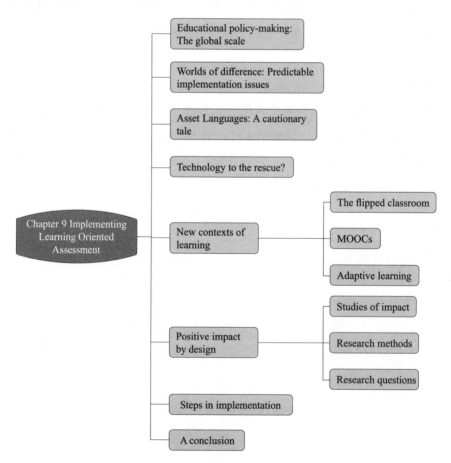

图 9.1 第九章思维导图目录

2. 表格呈现本章目录

表 9.1　第九章表格目录

9 Implementing Learning Oriented Assessment	第九章 实施面向学习的测评
EDUCATIONAL POLICY-MAKING: THE GLOBAL SCALE	9.1 教育政策制定：全球范围
WORLDS OF DIFFERENCE: PREDICTABLE IMPLEMENTATION ISSUES	9.2 世界的不同：可预测的实施问题
ASSET LANGUAGES: A CAUTIONARY TALE	9.3 语言资产：一个警示故事
TECHNOLOGY TO THE RESCUE?	9.4 依靠技术来拯救？
NEW CONTEXTS OF LEARNING The flipped classroom MOOCs Adaptive learning	9.5 学习的新环境 　9.5.1 翻转课堂 　9.5.2 慕课 　9.5.3 适应性学习
POSITIVE IMPACT BY DESIGN Studies of impact Research methods Research questions	9.6 设计积极影响 　9.6.1 影响研究 　9.6.2 研究方法 　9.6.3 研究问题
STEPS IN IMPLEMENTATION	9.7 实施步骤
A CONCLUSION	9.8 结语

补充思考题及参考作答

1. 请列出本书中引用的杜威的所有名言、名句及出处。你最喜欢其中的哪一句，为什么？如果让你选择，你最希望阅读杜威的哪部著述，为什么？

参考作答 1

（1）本书引用的杜威的名言名句如下：

Chapter One：It requires troublesome work to undertake the alteration of old beliefs.

How We Think

(John Dewey 1933:29-30)

Chapter Two：The value of any fact or theory as bearing on human activity is, in the long run, determined by practical application--that is by using it for accomplishing some definite purpose.

What Psychology Can Do for the Teacher

(John Dewey and Alexander McLellan, 1908:195)

Chapter Three：Education is a social process; education is growth; education is not preparation for life but is life itself.

My Pedagogical Creed

(John Dewey, 1897)

Chapter Four：There's all the difference in the world between having something to say and having to say something.

The School and Society

(John Dewey 1915:35)

Chapter Five：The goal of education is to enable individuals to continue their education.

Democracy and Education

(John Dewey, 1916:100)

Chapter Six：Were all instructors to realize that the quality of mental process, not the production of correct answers, is the measure of educative growth something hardly less than a revolution in teaching would be worked.

Democracy and Education

(John Dewey, 1916:183)

Chapter Seven：Give the pupils something to do, not something to learn and the doing is of such a nature as to demand thinking; learning naturally results.

Democracy and Education

(John Dewey, 1916:160)

Chapter Eight：The two limits of every unit of thinking are a perplexed, troubled, or confused situation at the beginning, and a cleared up, unified, resolved situation at the close.

How We Think

(John Dewey, 1933:106)

Chapter Nine：A problem well put is half solved.

Logic: Theory of Inquiry

(John Dewey, 1938:108)

（2）我最喜欢的一句是 "The goal of education is to enable individuals to continue their education." (John Dewey, 1916:100)。这句话的意思是教育的目的是使个体能继续自我教育。正如这次导读活动，我们经历了关于测试领域新知识的洗礼，接受了辜老师专业的导读指导，学习到了阅读和搜索文献专著等一些技巧，这些将对我们未来的科研教学有所帮助。我们通过运用这些知识和技巧，继续科研和教学。这不正是这次导读活动的目的吗？

（3）希望阅读的专著：昨晚在阅读完第九章后，在网上买了杜威的两本专著 *How We Think* 和 *Democracy and Education*。因为有太多的困惑，想看看杜威自己是如何理解这些名言名句的，可能还会再买英译版，自我感觉理解能力有限，想看看一些专家学者的理解。从本书作者的引用来看，作者阅读的专著很多，这也在提醒自己，做科研和教学，需要不断提升自己的理论储备，升华思维高度。要给学生一杯水，自己就要有一桶水。假如自己不进步，如何鼓励学生进步呢？正所谓学高为师，身正为范。

参考作答 2

（1）我喜欢第三章中 "Education is a social process; education is growth; education is not preparation for life but is life itself." 教育是一个社会化过程；教育即成长；教育不是为了生活，是生活本身。喜欢这种终身学习的教育理念，把生活与教育

融为一体。第五章中 "The goal of education is to enable individuals to continue their education."（教育的目的是使个体能够继续他们的教育。）教育是终身的，就像生活要继续一样。正如这次辜老师领我们进行的导读活动一样，这是一个社会化的教育过程，也是所有参与者的成长过程。在此过程中，我们收获的不仅仅是书本的知识和理念，更学会了相关的技能和方法，例如如何查找文献，如何从教学和实践中寻找科研方向，如何学会学习。我们一点点改变着自己的行为，进而改变着我们的思维，这是教育、是成长，也是我们的生活。相信即使此次活动结束，我们从中获得的技能和能力也会对我们今后的学习、工作、科研产生深远的影响。为了后续的阅读和思考，我已经购买了辜老师推荐的几本书和杜威的几本著作，要好好研读。

（2）希望读的著作：我想读 *How We Think* 这本书，因为"如何思考"一直是我想了解又一直不懂的问题。

参考作答 3

（1）最喜欢的一句话是 "The two limits of every unit of thinking are a perplexed, troubled, or confused situation at the beginning, and a cleared up, unified, resolved situation at the close." 这句话揭示了思维的过程，最初大部分都是以迷惑开始，最后以清晰结束。

（2）希望读的著作：*How We Think*。

2. 作者为什么会在本章中引用杜威名言 (A problem well put is half solved.)？请遴选一个你在本书阅读过程中提出的好问题 / 思考题和一个导读过程中辜老师提出的你认为好的补充思考题。请问两者之间有什么共性？

参考作答 1

杜威有句名言 "A problem well put is half solved."（如果问题设计得好，就相当于已经解决了一半）。个人认为"问题设计"不仅仅指题目本身，也包括与应用实施相关的一系列条件，这些都是需要设计的，也是设计问题的时候需要考虑在内的。以本章为例，LOA 本身的构成及其实施的条件都是作者需要考虑的问题，而它对于所有目标读者来说也有同样的要求，既要了解 LOA，又要了解实施 LOA 相关的一切条件、原则以及方法和步骤。

我认为在阅读中自己提的比较好的思考题是阅读第一章时提出的问题："作者第一章第二页原文 Learning Oriented Assessment as presented in this volume offers a vision of radical change and far more effective learning。首次提到 LOA 时，既没有解释什么是 LOA，也没有解释 LOA 提供了一种 radical change 以及 far more effective learning 中 radical 从何而来，more effective 是相对于什么来说的呢？LOA 作为全书的重点，这种处理是不是就是一种缺陷和不足呢？"

我认为辜老师提出的非常好的思考题很多，但是我想举出其中一个最具代表性的（对第一、第二章补充的思考题），"请结合你的学习、工作或生活经历，谈谈你对作者引用的杜威的话的理解。"

两者之间的共性在于，自从这两个问题提出来之后，我在全书的阅读中一直在有意识地注意这两个问题，或者在试图找到问题的答案。这两个问题贯穿我阅读的始终，而且一直在引领我思考。我自己的问题主要针对本书，老师的问题把本书与我们的工作、学习和生活都结合起来了，正体现了"教育本身就是生活"的理念。

参考作答 2

我认为这句话涵盖了如何实施 LOA 的本质，即实施 LOA 在很多方面激励我们去提出好问题以及解决好这些问题。

我提出的好问题：Learning for mastery 中 mastery 的程度是什么呢？完全掌握吗？知识是层层递进，先分块掌握再整合，或者先浅显再深奥，"完全"到哪一种地步呢？这个是否与阶段学习目标相结合？那么在判定是否达标时，用不用 test 或者 assessment 呢？如果用的话，会不会最后出现 learning for tests？

辜老师提出的好问题：你赞同测评是一种学习模式吗？为什么？

共性：1）这两个问题都是在连环问，连环问能促进我去思考"为什么我要那样思考"，这个于我有益。2）二者都需要作者引用文献再发表观点，融入他人观点后提出新看法，这是重要的学术能力。

3. 你认为本章的写作思路如何体现 LOA 所倡导的系统性、生态性和社会认知性？

参考作答

　　构建了"四个世界"，并将四者以"任务"为驱动形成环状，以服务于"学习"的目的。这"四个世界"为"个人""教育""社会""测评"，分别代表个人认知的发展、课程学习、社会技能和专门语言技能的获取、测评任务的构建。"个人"运用"任务"发展个体的认知；"教育"运用"任务"设计课堂练习、组织正式教学；"社会"运用"任务"评价技能表现；"测评"以"任务"为测量基础。通过"任务"驱动实现了两种方式的"学习"：在现实世界中通过参与"任务"实现自然习得（natural acquisition）和在正式教育环境中通过接受教育实现学习。通过"四个世界"，个人、教育、社会、测评构成了一个连贯的有机体，体现了 LOA 的系统性和生态性。"四个世界"也体现了 LOA 的社会认知性，例如，个人为了获得进入社会所需要的技能，可以通过接受教育获得认知的发展，实现学习的进步。LOA 对学习的诠释体现了教育的本质：学习不只发生在课堂，而应贯穿学习者的一生。

4. 你认为 9.2（pp.123-125）中指出的 13 点 LOA 实施过程中需要解决的问题（请再认真阅读），哪些是我们作为教师/学生个体可以解决的？如何解决？

参考作答 1

　　（1）第 1、3、7、8、10、11 点：教师对"形成性评估"理念及实践的理解，教师对"形成性评估"和"终结性评估"的区分，教师对自身角色的理解以及教师实施形成性评估的能力培养能够通过自我教育、学习培训和实践尝试来解决。

（2）第9、12点：教师解决了自身在评估方面存在的问题才能真正地关注学习，主动进行对学生能力的培养。

（3）第2、4、5、13点：需要决策部门的大力参与和推动。

（4）第6点：关于课程以及评估程序等作为教师的我们在某种程度上有一定的自主权，但是也需要协调规划。

参考作答 2

第一个问题是关于决策者的，第二个问题也是关于决策者的，第三个问题是关于测评专家的，第四个至第七个问题是教师和学生可以努力的。

具体做法：教师提升自己的评价素养，努力理解形成性评价、区分形成性评价和终结性评价，向其他实施形成性评价的学校学习经验，并创造性地应用到自己的课堂，尽力使之发挥积极作用，避免终结性评价在自己的课堂一统天下。第八个问题是教师教育，高校教师可以在自己的课堂努力培养师范生的测评素养。第九个问题是关于教师的，教师可以尝试使用面向学习的测评从而调整自己的教学实践。第十个问题是关于大众意识，这个可以依赖个体和团体进行宣传。

5. 9.3（p.125）中的 Asset Languages 是一个什么计划 / 项目？它的失败给我们的启示 / 教训是什么？

参考作答 1

Asset Languages 项目简介：

Asset Languages (AL) emerged from the UK's National Languages Strategy, launched in 2002 to address serious problems in language education. The strategy included the Languages Ladder, a new voluntary recognition system. AL, the assessment system developed to deliver it, is a framework for lifelong learning encompassing six levels and 25 languages. AL took the Common European Framework of Reference for Languages (CEFR) as an important point of reference, and has relevance as a case study, both for what we did and did not use of the pilot Manual. Our approach was determined above all by the need to impose consistency across languages in the way scales were constructed and levels determined. We describe our approaches to objectively and subjectively assessed skills, explaining where we followed the pilot Manual and other procedures we used. We argue that the Manual should encourage methodological innovation, and also that CEFR linking procedures should be seen as integral to test construction and administration, rather than a one-off exercise. （Asset languages: A case study of piloting the CEFR Manual）

启示：该项目的失败告诉我们任何项目，无论有多好，其价值体现在能够为目标用户服务。对于教育项目来说，教育决策者、学校负责人和教师三者达成共识并一致致力于项目实践的实施才有可能达到项目预期的效果。

参考作答 2

Asset Languages 是一个以交际能力为目标的改革，但是它失败了。作者陈述它失败的原因是：1）没有重新聚焦使用语言的目的是交际；2）没有把理念传递给潜在参与者，比如教师和学校领导者。

失败的启示：实施 LOA 得先让使用者和参与者明白实施 LOA 的价值在哪里，再整合课程设计者、教师团体、测评专家，同心协力。

6. 你在教学中最成功的技术应用有哪些？

参考作答 1

这学期（2020 年春季学期）线上教学之前，我所用的技术应该就是局限于用电脑播放课件和视频等。这学期因为线上教学要求使用学习通，虽然这个 App 还有很多不足，但是我发现其中的讨论功能很好用，有点类似于论坛。我可以将课堂讨论题放在讨论里，要求学生分享自己的看法并评论至少两个同学的看法。虽然大多数同学只是很简单地评论，或者有的可能只是应付性地评论，但是我也看到了一些同学闪光的观点，得到了一些他们阅读他人观点的证据。这极大地弥补了线下教学时学生不参与或者没有时间参与到讨论环节中的缺陷（课堂讨论环节时，很多同学实际上都是在做自己的事情，每次真正参与进去的就那么几个固定的同学），也给予了一些在课堂讨论时羞于表达的同学表达的机会。我认为，这算是一个比较好的技术，虽然还只是初步尝试，但我相信学生的表现会越来越好！

这学期我新带了一门英语写作课，我让学生对写作做 peer review，教他们如何使用 word 里面的批注功能和修订功能。同学们说这是他们第一次做这种活动，很多同学也是第一次使用 word 的这种功能，虽然结果还没出来，但是我相信学生在这一过程中的收获肯定不仅停留在写作方面。

我还计划在这门课程讲到应用文写作时，让他们使用真正的邮箱互相写email，相信应该也会很有意思。

参考作答 2

微课、慕课、翻转课堂、网络平台以及课堂直播已经依次走入我们的教学，占据着很重要的位置。所谓成功可能是当时觉得很好，但是现在看来缺乏科学合理的设计，这是今后要用心改进的地方。

7. 如今的学习生态与十年前相比有什么根本性的不同？但哪一点或在哪些方面是亘古不变的？

参考作答

根本变化在于网络环境的出现、学习方式和内容的改变。十年前的学习大部分来自于学校教育，学习者坐在教室中，教师在三尺讲台上传授知识，使用的教学设备大部分都是简单的黑板、粉笔、纸质练习册和纸质教科书。现如今，伴随着科技的发展和移动设备的普及，移动学习走进了千家万户。学习不再受制于传统的课堂，移动学习打破了时间和地点的限制，只需要一台移动设备和网络就可以实现随时随地的学习。这极大地改变了学习方式，混合学习、翻转课堂、慕课的涌现使得移动学习欣欣向荣。同时，移动学习网络空间中存储的大量学习资源也让学习触手可及，极大地丰富了学习者学习的内容。

即学习者技能的获得与能力的培养，进而实现社会价值。

8. 请查阅和分享 Nick Saville 的文献，阅读其摘要和文献中的图表，结合本章 9.6 谈谈你对 positive impact by design 的认识及其在我们的教学中如何应用。

参考作答

"Positive impact by design" 即评估实体在设计评估时要全面考虑评估的目的、评估的形式、评估的题目设计、受试群体、对测试者和受试者的能力要求、数据的收集与解析、评估的预期结果、评估反馈、评估结果的使用以及评估的影响等，尽最大可能减小或者消除消极的影响，扩大积极影响。

我们在教学中的评估也要充分考虑各种可能因素，使评估最大限度地为教学、为促学服务，使评估真正成为学习的一部分。

9. Figure 9.1 Steps in implementation 作者是从测试研发机构的视角出发，如果从我们一线教师或学习者的视角出发，实施的步骤与作者在 Figure 9.1 中的步骤会有什么异同？

参考作答

如果从一线教师或学者的角度出发，步骤应该是 Practice obstacles or implications—theory—implementation—practice—feedback。

相同之处：9.7 Steps in implementation 从测试研发机构的视角出发，步骤为 1. Stance—2. Language policy—3. A theory of action—4. The vision—5. Development, implementation—6. Progress monitoring—7. Outcomes evaluated against goals. 在这些步骤当中，包含教师实施 LOA 的环节。

不同之处：从测试研发机构出发，其步骤主要包括从科研机构出发研发的测评原则，到政府制定语言政策，到教师了解理论，到具体的实施，如：教师培训、课程发展、测评、影响研究，这些是完整的流程；其中，作为一线教师或者是学习者，主要集中于 LOA 在教学当中的测评。

10. 本章结论 / 结语为什么是 "A conclusion" 而不是我们通常所见的 "Conclusions"？

参考作答

　　本章的结语是 "A conclusion" 而不是常见的 "Conclusions" 是因为本章最后归结了一个结论，即通过阅读本书，读者将意识到 "the key skills which make good learners are transferrable across subject disciplines"，那么教育的目的就是 "Education is not about the transmission of content, but about changing the person, and equipping them to continue their development in the world beyond school."

11. 请翻译本章也是本书最后一段文字。请问哪些关键能力是好的学习者共通的可迁移的能力？我们怎样培养这些能力？

参考作答 1

　　撰写本书时，我们着眼于语言教育，但是在这项研究过程中最大的收获是，我们切身意识到，作为一个优秀学习者，关键技能是学科间的触类旁通。再一次说明一个显而易见却又往往被遗忘的事：教育不是知识的传递，而是改变人，通过武装人的头脑，让他离开学校后，在社会上继续学习和发展。

　　好的学习者共通的可迁移能力包含：学习能力、批判性思维、创造性思维、沟通能力、合作能力、社会责任。首先，学习能力能够使学习者保持不断学习的状态，更新自身的知识库。在校期间的教育使得学习者学习到了专业的知识，同时不断形成自我学习能力，拥有学习能力，即使踏出校门，忘记自身的专业知识，也能继续在社会上学习和发展。其次，批判性思维和创造性思维也是必备能力。这两者可以确保学习者保持自身独立思想，不随波逐流，不人云亦云。然后，沟通能力、合作能力和社会责任都是人处于社会之中的必备能力。无论是学习、工作还是生活，我们都需要不断地与人相处，具备沟通能力、合作能力和社会责任有助于我们更好地实现自身的价值，更好地为社会和国家的发展做贡献。

　　要想培养这些能力，我们可以把学校教育、家庭教育和社会教育相结合，三方同时发力，共同培养。

参考作答 2

本书把语言教育作为研究重点，但是它为我们提供的最有价值的启示在于，使我们意识到成为好的学习者的核心素养是可以跨学科迁移。最明显又最容易被忽略的是：教育不是学习内容的传递，而是要使学习者通过教育发生改变，从而具备在学校之外的现实世界继续成长的能力。

好的学习者共通的可迁移能力包含：独立和批判性思考的能力、沟通能力、与他人合作的能力和解决问题的能力等。

怎样培养这些能力：凡事不要简单地问一个 what，而是要问 why。

12. 本期导读第三阶段"扩展阅读、思考与实践"，请问你希望 / 期待如何进行？

参考作答 1

期待第三阶段：1）讨论以 LOA 为中心；2）每天有问题可以回答（很希望到第三阶段能够自问自答并分享）；3）期待和老师还有大家在群里讨论。

参考作答 2

我个人期待扩展阅读以本书为参考，利用前期搜索的资料，具体尝试如何进行文献阅读、思考与实践。如何阅读文献，看看我们以前的文献阅读方法到底对不对，从辜老师的著作导读，我意识到了自己的很多不足，改正了以前的不好习惯。特别感谢辜老师！期待扩展阅读更多的精彩！

附录
Appendix

《面向学习的测评：一种系统的方法》活动
第一阶段"总引"线上答疑

本次线上答疑采用现场提问、现场解答的方式。除了"总引"部分的内容，读者提问还涉及学习、研究的方法等多个方面。辜向东教授、贝尔法斯特女王大学在读博士生李玉龙（本期所读专著的书评和导读合作者）和中国矿业大学李廉老师（辜老师编外指导的青年教师）进行了解答。

第一阶段答疑音频
（扫码保存可听）

1. 关于写书评方面，我感觉不知道怎么下手，想请教您和其他老师以下问题。

1）书评有没有什么格式和结构要求？

2）是否需要旁征博引来支撑观点和论据？

3）我看了您分享的研究生写书评的总结，感觉理论基础不需要太高也可以尝试写书评，是吗？

4）有人说，写得好的文献应该很容易看懂，不那么拗口，而不是术语堆砌，您觉得是这样的吗？

5）读经典很重要，但现在的书太多了，很难选择。如果有经典导读的书单就好了。

辜向东：

1）每个发表书评的期刊都有具体要求。

2）因为篇幅有严格限制，不能旁征博引。但写作者起码要读几轮文献：（1）专著；（2）专著作者相关文献；（3）其他学者相关文献；（4）目标期刊样本书评 5~10 篇。

3）研究生能够写作书评并发表，基本上要有阅读上百篇高水平期刊文献的基础，尽管很多文献他们未必真读懂、读透了。不论能否发表，我个人认为书评写作是学术起步训练的第一步。

4）读懂、读通、读透一本好书是最基本的要求。越是深入浅出越能彰显水平。重要的是在做中学。

5）选择不难，看自己领域和相关领域的高水平期刊文章，最佳著作奖、最佳论文奖获得者的著述，最高水平会议主旨发言人的著述和终身成就奖、杰出成就奖获得者的著述。真正难的是坚持每天输入，让输入同吃饭睡觉一样，成为必须。

2. 我一直有个困惑，虽然读到研三了，但是自己很少写东西，导致现在自己在写作方面有很严重的畏难情绪和不自信，写作任务也会拖延。所以想请教您怎么才能解决这个问题？

辜向东：

这个问题比较具有共性。关于输入和输出严重不足的问题非常具有普遍性。我的一个比较实际的建议是：第一，养成写日记的习惯（中文英文都可以）。第二，写读书笔记。看一篇文章一定要写东西，提一些问题，做一些总结。坚持每天都做一些，可以读英文文献，用汉语写读书笔记，以帮助内化和转化，检验读懂多少。第三，要实践，找到一个研究点，然后扩展，比如写综述或做实证研究。

3. 如何取得书评写作授权？能否请您分享国际专著书评写作的申请步骤，向出版社还是向作者申请？国内发表书评需要授权吗？

李玉龙：

第一，关于如何取得书评写作授权。首先作者必须得找到书评主编的邮箱，但有些时候期刊网站不会直接把书评主编的邮箱挂出来，这时我们可以通过其他途径间接联系上书评主编。以 *Innovations in Education and Teaching International* 为例，期刊在 Editorial Board 中留了助理编辑的邮箱，这时我们不妨先试着联系一下。申请书评授权一般包括以下内容：自我介绍（身份介绍、相关成果与优势简介），对书的内容与价值进行简介，表达申请授权的意愿（含可以交稿的期限，一般 2~4 周）。总体而言，邮件既要热情诚恳，又要体现出自身优势与书的价值。一般而言，对方会在 2 周之内回复，如果没回复可能对方太忙或者在休假，当然极少数期刊压根就不会回复。如果对方回复，一般就会授权。如果不回复，我们还是要尝试再联系一下，把先前的邮件也一并抄送。需要注意的是，和书评主编或助理编辑联系前，要斟酌文字，尽量不要出现语法错误，如果可能，最好找团队反馈一下。

第二，关于书评写作的申请步骤，首先要第一时间获得好书（关注出版社、研究领域、学术会议），拿到书阅读，接着评估书评可以在哪些期刊发表，然后和书评主编联系获取授权（介绍自己、书的特点、强项能力）。

第三，国内发表书评一般不需要授权，可以关注期刊的要求。

4. 能否分享您日常比较固定的文献获取、阅读、研究产出以及合作交流的经验？

辜向东：

硕士期间，我没有研究意识。在读博期间，一年读了二三十本语言测试方面的专著，当时以读专著为主。我的学术起步于博士阶段，第一学期读语言学专著，要写 6 篇课程论文，基本保持每天读 100 页的文献。我建议大家：

1）关于文献获取，专著和期刊文献要同步进行。即使读不懂也是一种收获，只有这样才会让自己明白差距在哪里。

2）关于阅读，要自己输入，与导师和团队讨论交流。全职硕士一周读 5 篇高水平文献；博士则每天两三篇高水平文献；在职老师每周至少用两个半天读两篇高水平文献。要摸索建立自己的书单。

3）关于研究产出，在输入过程中我们一定要带着问题去阅读，一个很重要的学术研究的起步就是要学会思考、学会提问题、学会质疑、学会挑战权威。

4）建立自己的学术共同体，比如导师、同门、校友、同事、参加学术会议所认识的人，都有可能发展成你的学术共同体。

5. 请问 assessment 和 measurement 的区别在哪篇文章或著作中有提及？

李廉：

前面有老师说到 assessment 和 measurement 的区别：见到放在一起比较的概念有 assessing、testing、evaluation 三个。这种区分比较常见，Bachman 的研究比较有代表性，在 20 世纪八九十年代，他专门作过 testing、assessing、measuring 的区分，感兴趣的老师可以查一下他 1990、1993、1996 的系列书。但在他的 2010 年著名的《语言测评实践：现实世界中的测试开发与使用论证》中，提到了这三者在应用中没多大区别，在行为体系、实证手段、方法论和存在基础（grounding）上都相同。这是一个宽容的态度，我认为这是必要的。在进行研究、论述时需要这么一个宽容的态度，个别特殊情况可以再作区分，甚至求助于词典。

对于它们和 evaluation，一般认为是有区别的，比如 Bachman 说过，evaluation 是在 assessing 基础上的使用行为，是一种决策行为（参见《语言测评实践：现实世界中的测试开发与使用论证》的测试开发和使用流程图），它比前几者更"语用"。国内也比较多：刘润清老师（《语言测试和它的方法（修订版）》中就有，我看的第一本语言测试书）、韩宝成老师也在多个场合里作过区分，仅在讲座上我就听过两三次，论文记得也是有的。总的来说，国内学者们趋向于"区分"这三个概念：大约是 assessing 在行为上比 testing 更大，收集证据范围更广，后者是"测"，前者还包含了"评"，而 evaluation 争议不大，国内外基本一致。

Measurement 与它们放在一起比较，我见得相对少一些，国内外都是，在教育测量中这个词和 monitoring 倒是常放在一起比较，但实际上它是应该在上述比较行列的，心理测量和心理测试就是经常被带在一起的概念。我见过的有 Bachman 的专门论述：measuring 和 assessing 没什么区别（《语言测评实践：现实世界中的测试开发与使用论证》），我个人表示认同。

6. 导读部分提到 LOA 是基于《欧框》确立的，《欧框》已经是一个很完备的体系了，有根据它所开发的有影响力的考试和教材，我们中国现在有了《中国英语能力等级量表》，但是相配套的体系还有待完善。在现阶段，请问我们一线老师如何更科学地将 LOA 用于教学实践？

辜向东：

先简单回应一下，等读完整本书我们再来一起探讨。第一，建议阅读《欧框》（2001 版和 2018 版）；第二，把《中国英语能力等级量表》当作工具书一样，能从头到尾地通览，而且用里面的量表做教师自评、学生自评和教师评价；第三，阅读《欧框》的相关应用研究文献，与《中国英语能力等级量表》结合起来应用在教学实践和研究当中。

7. 作为教师，我最关注的问题是：如何把测试与英语教学相结合，如何以评促学、以评促教？国外关于将《欧框》应用于教学实践的文献多吗？

辜向东：

我们国家有深厚的测试文化，很多人都说测试的负面影响，这个我表示反对，尤其高考和大学英语四、六级考试，大家觉得是指挥棒。我想问的是，它们真的是指挥棒吗？我们的教学真的是在围着这些指挥棒转吗？不是的。我举个例子：我和一位中学老师 2019 年发表的关于 2018 年高考阅读分析的文章。我们查了高考阅读文章的来源（*Daily Express, The Economists, Science, NutriSpeak, Reader's Digest, SlideShare, Beijing Review, The Christian Science Monitor* 等），很多时候，我们看到的是形式而不是内容。如果中学老师和学生平时阅读的都是原汁原味的文章，考试就不成问题。考试是抽样，如果我们真正教好、学好了是不怕被抽和测试的。关于《欧框》的文献相当多。我提一个建议：如果要做实证研究，可以尝试做二语习得方面的复制性研究，就是找到非常好的 sample paper，去模仿，做复制性研究。

8. **书上强调学习是在社会文化互动的过程中完成的，我在吴岩司长关于"新文科，新外语"的报告中看到，现在外语教学也强调融入中国文化元素，服务国家战略。这种跨文化交际，特别是文化输出的能力要如何通过测评有效培养呢？**

辜向东：

我举两个例子。比如文化自信，可以分享各国领导人的富有思想和内容的新春致辞音频和文本，让学生阅读，多方面地去看这些材料，做各种对比，语言的、内容的、逻辑的，等等，并对国际关系等进行讨论，可以用于对学生的过程性评价。又如，现在我们强调思政教育，可以对领导人讲话的中英文稿、政府工作报告的中英文稿等进行学习，让学生对当前和未来的事情有所了解，培养他们的参与意识和国际视野。

9. 我对如何通过阅读文献来形成自己的研究过程还不是很清楚。我的问题是：我们是应该有了自己的想法，然后从文献中找证据来塑造自己研究的论证，还是应该在阅读中积累研究的想法？如果是后者，那么我们该怎么做才能避免在读了很多文献之后不知所云，迷失在别人一个又一个严密的论证中？

辜向东：

我觉得这个问题没有先后，可以从教学和学习当中的问题和困惑开始，也可以通过读文献发现问题开始。如果是从读文献开始，有一个很重要的地方需要特别注意，尤其是国外高水平文献，就是文章最后一般都会提到本研究的问题和不足，这些往往就是给我们指出了未来发展研究的方向或者研究的一些选题。如果从实践出发，就要 evidence-based，用事实说话。以我的第一篇实证研究文章为例，我在教学中发现词汇是学生存在的普遍问题，就去思考和研究大纲和教材中对此是如何呈现的，接着在学生和教师中做调查，然后结合文献，形成了我的第一篇实证研究文章。

在读博之前，我就发现中国的母语教育和外语教育都非常重视精读，但对泛读很不重视，于是我在读博期间写了一篇语言测试课程论文"在四、六级考试中增加快速阅读的必要性"，后来四、六级考试增加了快速阅读，应该说 original idea 就来自我那篇课程论文。这就说明，我们可以从很多方面去找研究的点。如果你从文献开始，阅读一定要比较 focus，比如 *Language Assessment Quarterly* 的特色栏目名家访谈，阅读名家著述，访谈者的文献，训练自己写文献综述。还有一点就是，大家在生活当中要透过现象看本质，一定要把看到的东西和自己的研究结合起来。比如我们团队两个国家社科课题分别产生于大学英语四、六级考试监考过程中和看电视上关于改革开放三十周年的新闻，它们都是在生活当中发现的。

10. 能分享一下您提到的两位老师申请博士的经历吗？

辜向东：

第一，要过语言关，语言是第一关。语言学习我不赞同高分低能的说法，世界上没有哪一所好的大学是不以分数取人的，比如剑桥入学，雅思要求 7.5，多数被录取者达到 8 分、8.5 分，甚至 9 分。分数是准入条件，只不过分数不是他们取人的唯一标准。

第二，要做好学术准备，起码要花三年时间，阅读文献、参加会议、发表文章等。

第三，要锁定学校、导师，通过读文献、参加学术会议、建立学术联系等。

第四，要撰写 research proposal，包括明确的研究问题、文献综述以及研究思路。另外还有面试等。

11. 如果把自己定位成一个职前的中学英语教师，硕士阶段三年在语言测试方面应该将 focus 放在哪里呢？应该多去中学英语课堂观察，找到想要研究的问题，还是应该从文献出发，梳理出能够为中学英语课堂提供帮助的 evidence？

辜向东：

看国内外与中小学相关的文献，结合自己的教学经验与同事的经历，看看能做什么研究。大学研究的研究思路和方法可以迁移到对中小学的研究当中。

12. 对于中学英语老师，做科研应该从哪儿做起呢？

辜向东：

中学老师研究的点是很丰富的，理论要求不那么高，在期刊发文章相对来说不是那么难。我的建议是，以教学中的问题为导向，关注学生的真正阅读，比如教材的利用率,可参考辜向东等(2011)《课改进程中的高中英语教学现状探究》一文。再比如中学的课堂管理,很多英语课堂不是在教阅读,学生的真正阅读很少,学生的输入和思考很少,那么如何去改变?我认为外语教育有两个很简单的衡量标准:第一,学生原汁原味语言材料输入的质与量;第二,有效产出的质与量。可参考辜向东等(2019)《CSE阅读量表在高中生自我评价中的有效性及影响因素》一文。当然,也要有一定的文献输入,中学老师是完全可以做研究的。

13. 近年二语习得实证研究对研究方法、研究数据分析这块要求很高,很专业,有时还不容易看懂。您有没有好的方法和建议?

辜向东:

研究方法不应该成为我们的障碍,因为方法其实都是成熟的,最重要的是你要解决什么问题。如果方法上遇到困难,可以找合作者,当然自己会更好。自己学会有很多途径,我们有很多网课,比如出版社会定期邀请专家讲研究方法,国内也有很多关于研究方法的线下研修班,也有很多关于研究方法的著作。其实,最重要的还是看实证研究,去尝试做一些复制性研究。另外,可以找精通数据分析的人给你解释。不要有畏难情绪,要有breakthrough,硬着头皮往下看文献和尝试自己做研究。我建议,要学会一种方法,反复用它做研究。

14. 能分享一下怎么申请人文社科项目吗?如何让项目书吸引眼球?

辜向东:

可以看一些申请成功的项目论证书。我的国家社科基金一般项目和重点项目书之前都有分享。出版社也请我做过相关的讲座。申请国家社科基金项目一定要在比较高的层面:一是学术水准,二是要在国家层面关注(学科本身的发展和社会问题)。申请青年项目一般要有博士学位,除非选题特别好。具体来说:第一,前期研究基础很重要,可以从校内、市内课题做起,要有一些相关的文章发表;

第二，要有明确的研究方向，沿着某一领域，跟踪做五年、十年，精耕细作；第三，项目书一定要反复修改，一定要有一个团队，做到自己满意。自己满意的东西交出去才可能通过。

15. 您刚才说，文献综述可以给一些研究选题，可以深入讲一下吗？

辜向东：

这是一个非常有意义的研究的点。可以在自己感兴趣的某个领域做文献综述，比如大家参加了本期"我来读文献"活动，可以想想如何做 LOA 的文献综述，搜集 LOA 文献上百篇，要穷尽性搜集文献，集中阅读。再如，我们这个活动本身是不是可以做实证研究，可以跟踪每天大家对思考题的反馈，通过这些反馈可以发现很多问题，其实我们正在做的就是 LOA 的一个实践。我们用了很多其中的理论，比如社会建构主义理论，这就是我做这个导读用的理念，我们就是要构建一个学术共同体，大家在共同体当中有 conversation、communication、scaffolding。也可以设计问卷和访谈来调查大家从开始到结束的收获、体会、问题、困难等，我们甚至可以做一个系列研究出来，在某个期刊申请专栏，既有综述又有实证研究。

《面向学习的测评：一种系统的方法》活动
第二阶段"正文"线上答疑

第二阶段线上答疑采用现场提问、现场解答的方式。辜向东教授和特邀嘉宾本书第二作者 Nick Saville 博士进行了答疑，读者踊跃提问，讨论热烈。

1. In Chapter 9, Implementing Learning Oriented Assessment, how do the "examining body" and "language policy from the government" tell classroom teachers what to do and how to do in class to implement LOA?

辜向东：

我来简要介绍一下 Cambridge Assessment English 这个机构的一些背景和现在他们的考试在全球的使用，希望能帮助大家理解这一章（Chapter 9 Implementing Learning Oriented Assessment）关于 LOA 的实施情况。剑桥的系列考试以前主要是私立学校在使用，但是现在很多国家和地区的政府部门和教育部门接受了剑桥考试系列，并且在公立学校大规模使用。这样，剑桥考试的 stakeholders 以及实施的 contexts 就发生了很大变化。面对这样的新形势，他们作为考试研发机构，有义务和责任跟这些国家或地区的教育主管部门共同探讨如何面向学习进行测评。这是本书主要的出发点。另外，本书的两位作者先后在不同的国家或地区有过英语作为二语或者是外语的一线教学经历，比如 Nick Saville 博士就在日本、意大利、西班牙等国家和地区有过英语教学经历，他们比较了解课堂英语教学。

2. 读完本书，感觉触动最大的是我个人的思维，而不是实实在在的测试实践指导，所以这也是为什么最后一章只用了一个部分来说明实施的步骤，不知道我理解得有没有偏差？

辜向东：

是这样的，因为这本书的目的就是提出 LOA 这个理论框架，它是一个 action-oriented theory，重点不是讲具体怎么去实施，只有最后一章才是关于如何实施的。另外一点就是这里提到的思维，的的确确非常不一样。两位作者的写作思路更多的是提出观点，引导和促进大家阅读思考，具体每个实施的 context 不一样，LOA 理论框架只能作为具体实施的指导与参考。

3. 本书中 LOA 的实施借鉴了很多 formative assessment 和 AFL 的原则和方法，能够搜集到 LOA 的实证研究也非常有限，而学者们早在十几年前就提出来 LOA 的概念。所以，您如何看待 LOA 的发展和前景？

辜向东：

现在的 LOA 实证研究虽然不多，但还是有的，尤其是剑桥这个部门做了很多相关的实证研究。但是，因为这个机构主要是在做测评研发，发表论文不是第一要务，他们有很多研究是在学术会议上宣读的。另外大家可以关注一下他们的期刊 Research Notes，上面会有一些他们的实证研究。还有一点是他们与剑桥大学出版社联合推出了 Studies in Language Testing 系列（现在已经有 51 卷本），很多实证研究是作为 Book Chapters 收录在这个系列当中的。

一个新的理念的提出和人们对它的接受都有一个过程，更不要说实施，更何况 LOA 这个理念的实施涉及的 stakeholders 是全方位的，比如第九章讲实施就涉及 macro levels 和 micro levels 的各类利益相关群体。对于 LOA 的前景，在中国环境下，我个人非常希望能够看到我们每个个体能够做些什么样的改变。我想全世界也是这样的，我们不能等着决策部门、教育行政主管部门改变再去尝试，去实施。如果我们很多个体的力量能够汇聚在一起，就有可能产生很大的影响。

4. 请问剑桥商务英语考试与雅思考试有何不同？

辜向东：

这两个考试显然是很不同的。剑桥商务英语考试，首先它的研发最早是针对中国改革开放后，对外贸易的极大增长非常需要商务英语方面的人才的情形，是剑桥与教育部考试中心合作研发的。这个考试在中国实施成功后才扩展到其他国家和地区，在全球有较大影响力。剑桥商务英语考试分三个级别，对应《欧框》的 B1、B2、C1。每个级别的考生水平相对比较一致。现在英国和一些英联邦国家的高校也认可剑桥商务英语考试 C1 的成绩。雅思学术类考试主要是针对去英语或英联邦国家读本科、硕士、博士的学生的一个学术英语水平考试，考生的语言水平差异很大，雅思分为 1—9，不同的分数段与《欧框》的相应级别进行了对接，九级对应的应该是《欧框》的最高级 C2。

5. 请问对于暂时没有大规模考试和没有学科（ESP 中的 EOP）教学大纲的高职层次护理英语口语课程，是否可以展开 LOA？

辜向东：

对于很多高层次的护理人才来说，英语是他们就业的瓶颈，所以他们到海外去应聘比较困难，而全世界都非常需要这方面的护理人才。你们现在做的工作恰恰是有很大社会需求的。剑桥现在有针对医护人员的医学英语考试，是全球认可的，可以去关注一下。如果你们的学生能把这些考试作为其中的一个目标去提升他们的英语水平，那么他们是不愁就业的，而且会有非常好的就业前景。所以同样可以开展 LOA 的实践。

6. 我很赞同前面老师的观点，读了这本专著可以改变我们的思维。我觉得我对于学习的本质有了新的认识，对于如何评估学习也有了新的认识。于是我在思考，如何在教学中将学生培养成为成功的语言学习者？借着这学期全面网课的契机，如何为我所教授的课程搭建一个混合学习的模式？我感觉就可以借用本书第 7 章 Figure 7.1 的模型。我想听听辜老师的建议。

辜向东：

用这个模型去做教研的尝试，这个想法非常好。我们可以在第一阶段做个 pilot study，然后在这个基础上去总结。在第二阶段去正式实施，并在这个基础上做学术研究、发表论文、参加学术会议。有了前期的研究基础，就可以申请各级各类项目，尤其是教育部人文社科项目和国家社科基金项目，可以写作和出版专著。这就是学术的成长之路。另外，这些研究跟我们的教学紧密结合，反过来也能够有效地指导我们的教学实践，提升教学效果。

7. 我想了解一下，有没有具体介绍如何在 classroom level 实施 LOA 的书籍？

辜向东：

到目前为止，我所了解的好像还没有专著（但有学术文集正在编辑出版中），但是介绍如何实施的实证研究文章肯定有，大家可以搜索一下。

8. 英语核心素养中学习能力这一块，个人一直觉得很空很大，为此曾转向学习科学研究，结果更找不到方向了。然而，通过本次学习我发现，LOA 对英语学习能力培养研究很有价值，能否在二者的连接上给点启发呢？

辜向东：

关于这个 interface，我觉得可能第一步还是要在这两个方面去尝试查阅更多的文献，结合教学中的实际问题找到一个契合点，肯定是可以做研究的。

9. How do you think of the development and prospect of LOA as a theoretical framework for assessment?

Nick Saville:

Our approach is a very simple one really, trying to create a successful educational system in which all forms of assessment contribute to better learning, and in particular to prevent various forms of exams or high-stakes tests from having negative effects on learning, and what gets taught in classrooms.

I was interested to see that many of the questions have been about the figures and diagrams in the book, particularly questions about the arrows and directions in which they go. I think I need to point out that you need to be careful not to over-interpret the diagrams. I think in some cases there was a mistake leaving off one of the arrow points—in other words a printing error and not a feature of the diagram. They were all supposed to go both ways, but some only pointed one way. Perhaps I could use this opportunity to talk a bit more about the ways I would like you to read the diagrams more generally rather than to focus on the details.

The diagrams are basically there to indicate how a SYSTEM should be considered so that different components can all be linked up effectively. But the diagrams are not like a chemical formula or an engineering diagram which needs to be interpreted very precisely at the level of detail. You might say that the diagrams there are to help you to think about systems, rather than to tell you what a system should actually be like. After all, each local context is different, and all different components will need to work together in different ways.

Speaking of this, it takes me to the term "a systemic approach", which is the subtitle of the volume. It's precisely in this area and with this particular focus, that our conception of LOA differs from some of the emerging representations of the concept or the earlier descriptions, dating back to the early work of Purpura or Carless in Hong Kong, China.

You could say the diagrams in the book are only for providing general information—for referential purposes. They are there to help you to think about systems, not to give you the ready-made answer to what your local system needs to be like. They are the components of any educational context, but each educational context will have different ways in which those components come together—at both macro and micro levels.

Bear in mind that I write from the perspective of an exam provider. I believe exams can have a beneficial impact by design if they can be effectively aligned to learning and teaching goals.

10. In some contexts, exams have negative impacts, how can we avoid that?

Nick Saville:

LOA is my suggested answer to this dilemma. Always start with context and purpose and ensure that all forms of assessment are CONVERGENT. In other words, work hard to make sure that the most important educational goals remain central. But this convergence must be localized—macro and micro levels of both policy and practice should converge not diverge. LOA is a referential system in educational contexts, not a blueprint of the kind engineers uses. It is a systemic way of thinking about educational and other social processes that are dynamical and are always changing.

11. How can we align the actions of all stakeholders and maintain a change management perspective? What efforts are needed?

Nick Saville:

We need a referential system to guide actions. It is of course difficult, and you need to develop a theory of action in your context. Using ecological thinking is helpful. Ecologies are in a state of dynamic balance, always changing but not in chaos. Our job is to build ecologies that function well, and which can be changed effectively in response to a changing world. "Top down meets bottom up", it is about achieving equilibrium, while dealing with constant change. The book was intended to help people think about and implement solutions, like the CEFR.

12. In what ways do we say similar or different things than Carless? Turner and Purpura? And why?

Nick Saville:

Ours is a systemic approach. At the heart of it, we suggest that more people need to understand the conditions needed for successful language learning and how to achieve this is a systemic way. This also requires a deeper understanding of assessment and the roles it plays in learning—sometimes called language assessment literacy. You will, however, find many similarities in the work of Carless and in the recent publications of Turner and Purpura.

13. How do you define "successful" here?

Nick Saville:

Successful depends on the learning goal and whether you can build up enough evidence to show that the goal has been achieved. The experience and judgement of teachers are good, but it also needs validation like other forms of assessment—not just unsupported claims or opinions. Teaching skill is very important in classroom-based teaching and assessment. The question arises still: what evidence can be produced to show that the learning goals are being achieved? Being able to gather evidence (data of different kinds) is a necessary feature of LOA.

14. How do you come up with this LOA capitalized?

Nick Saville:

Neil Jones and I decided on the capitals to make people think about the specific features of our approach. It makes the title stand out and draws attention to the fact that our version of LOA may not be entirely the same as other conceptualizations.

15. What are your thoughts on assessment of learning compared with assessment for learning? What is the difference? How will you know by giving learners a task if they are learning what the theory predicts?

Nick Saville:

If you collect evidence to show that the learner has learned what she was intended to learn, that is evidence of learning. If you can use the same evidence to design a new learning task and set next step goals, that would be for learning. Note that the same evidence can be used for BOTH. Having said that, assessment procedures are often designed to maximize one or other of these functions.

The learner is the most important variable in understanding what is actually learning. Learning doesn't happen without motivation and purpose on the part of the learner—that is part of the theory. The learning task is at the center of our model. When learning and assessment tasks are convergent, it is possible to avoid some negative washback effects (such as cramming to pass tests without actually learning the language).

16. What are the new opportunities brought by new technologies and what are the possible ways to carry out?

Nick Saville:

Technology helps collect the evidence of and for learning. Teachers struggle to collect evidence and traditional exams on paper only collect narrow samples. Integration of learning and assessment (ILA) becomes possible with technology and offers some practical solutions that are viable. I am sure this will accelerate as a result of COVID-19. This current crisis is a fantastic opportunity to think constructively about how things can be better as a result (to achieve positive changes and better impact by design). But technology without theory is a problem, and the practical challenge is still very big—there is much work to be done!

17. Is effectiveness of technology–based learning or smart learning largely associated with effective assessment of that learning?

Nick Saville:

Too many apps that are emerging are useless for learning, just for fun perhaps.

Learning and assessment always go hand in hand but getting the integration right is the challenge. Learners will need guidance on accessing and using the right technology. Teaching will be more about supporting learning than providing content. Gamification still needs to be validated to show how engagement with the task helps the intended learning goals. My advice is to try not to "drown in information", but to use your theories and frameworks to evaluate the options available. Make reasoned choices and evaluate what you are doing. Use all forms of data that can be collected to inform you and to work out what works well—and what doesn't. Collaborate with others in this to build a better picture across many local contexts.

《面向学习的测评：一种系统的方法》活动 第三阶段线上答疑

第三阶段线上答疑采用现场提问、现场解答的方式。辜向东教授和特邀嘉宾本书第二作者 Nick Saville 博士进行了答疑，现场讨论热烈。

1. My question is about the task in the LOA paradigm. From p.137 we know that "tasks must have interactional authenticity, that is, learners' cognition is engaged on the communicative task at hand, not on winning a positive appraisal of performance". My question is: In the classroom where English is taught as a foreign language, how to design interactional authentic tasks for learners? Could you give some examples for us?

Nick Saville:

There are two reasons for using a reference to Henry Widdowson (e.g., *Teaching Language as Communication*, 1978) to address some questions I have received. The first is that the origins of LOA are in the communicative approach to teaching and learning. What Widdowson wrote about in the 1970s and 1980s is still true for me (e.g., use vs. usage). The second is that Widdowson discussed authenticity and was one of the first authors to explore the concept of interactional authenticity.

Since the 1990s (see Bachman, 1990, Chapter 8), we have understood the need for learning and assessment tasks to have both situational and interactional authenticity (Bachman & Palmer, 1996; Douglas, 2000; Weir, 2005), stimulating test-takers to engage with the task rather than simply show language knowledge (usage). As I say, this view dates back to the writings of Widdowson in the early days of the communicative approach from the mid-1970s onwards (see also Widdowson 1979; 1983). You might like to check out other references from that era. The context of situation (Firth) is the starting point of any communicative event. A task therefore needs situational authenticity. This is provided by Can-do descriptors and other features of the context that can be created for pedagogic purposes (see Council of Europe on the *Threshold Level*, 1975 and *Wilkins' Functional/Notional Syllabus*, 1976).

I received a question about the audience for our LOA book. It was written for a general academic audience interested in learning, teaching and assessment of languages. We wanted to keep it concise and accessible in the way it was written. We didn't write the book specifically for teachers, but it can be used as part of teacher education or in-service training. Teachers need to understand the part that assessment plays in learning.

Luckily the book LOA has been introduced into China to make it available to a wider audience. The social context is the starting point of the action-oriented approach. But the model is actually a socio-cognitive one. The tasks for learning and assessment can be based on real-world tasks. That is the challenge for teachers and providers of learning materials. Task design is at the heart of LOA. In LOA we ask the question: How can all forms of assessment be designed to support learning? So, what about the assessment of lexical or grammatical knowledge [usage as Widdowson (1978:

15) called it]?

Teachers often try to use task-based language teaching in classroom, but sometimes it becomes task-supported language teaching—with a focus on form rather than functionality. I also understand that teachers, sometimes have to compromise authenticity to meet curriculum requirement set by policymakers.

2. So if the communicative task is at the heart of your pedagogy, when and where does the teaching of vocabulary fit in?

Nick Saville:

I suggest that you should think about the action-oriented approach at different levels of proficiency—you can use the CEFR or *China's Standards of English* (CSE) levels for this. What function (Can-do) are you focusing on in your lesson and what language resources are needed to complete the task?

The linguistic resources (e.g., vocabulary) can be introduced in various ways but need to be practiced in communicative events. To do this, we need to "extend the classroom" so that learning can take place before, during and after the lesson itself—and in particular, to ensure that there is enough time for practice. Our role as educators is to create a successful ecosystem of learning—to make connections and to motivate learners to USE the language for communication IN ORDER TO LEARN.

In your comments you seem to be agreeing that the learning of the vocabulary should improve the completion of the task—it is not an end in itself. So, if we want to assess grammar and lexis in order to support learning, we need to find the right way to do so. Context and purpose are essential considerations. If learners have a communication goal, they can develop the knowledge and skills to achieve that goal. That of course includes the words and structures needed.

The cognitive development of a language learner also includes the ability to retrieve and use words effectively for communicative purposes (e.g., in interactive conversations). Knowing the words (usage) does not guarantee an ability to USE them in "real time". To develop that ability requires practice in communicating. Of course, memorizing things is part of learning a language. Retrieving the knowledge and having it available for use is the problem. If the words are memorized out of context, many meanings that are learned may not be productive or helpful for communicating in speech.

The challenge is to create effective conditions for learning. LOA is an attempt to address that challenge by taking a systemic approach to the educational context. As stakeholders and participants in language education—as policymakers, teachers and assessment providers—we need to collaborate to create better conditions for learning for our learners.

3. Nick，how to design interactional authentic tasks for learners, could you give us some advice?

Nick Saville:

Tasks which engage the learner in solving a communication problem can be interactionally authentic. If you are at B1 level, a Can-do task might be to buy a ticket for a train. How could you develop a lesson plan and sequence of learning goals that enables the learner to engage in an interactionally authentic way? The context, purpose, motivation and engagement of the learner's cognition is important—not just an old-style role-play task. Careful design of the situational aspects of the task and consideration of how your learners should engage with it to learn or improve. The task is there to help the learner to learn something useful and to provide feedback for future learning. FEEDBACK is based on EVIDENCE. These are the two key components of assessment for learning within the LOA model: Engagement based on motivation and perseverance are central to learning. Technology helps make the connections and handles the collection and analysis of the evidence on behalf of the humans. The humans still need to design the tasks and use the feedback effectively. The machines do not take over the role of the teacher/assessor.

4. 首先感谢辜老师近段时间用心、专业、尽力、无私、热情的指导和分享，我现在特别想问：1）近段时间由于您的团队和各位群友的分享，我们积累了大量的中英文素材，一下子感觉太幸福。但是这么多宝贵的资料，又有些不知道该如何科学合理地阅读才能使这些材料真正地发挥其作用和价值。如何才能使它们不仅仅是一份材料，更是成为我们的知识积累和储备，真正地能为我们的教学和科研服务？关于这一点，您有什么建议？2）您觉得对于青年教师来说，考博是必须的吗？如果不考博，能否通过日常学习来补足？如何来补足？

辜向东：

我想这个问题比较具有共性，尤其是学术刚刚起步的老师，都觉得很容易被文献淹没。文献阅读具有选择性。这种选择性一定要在不断的实践摸索过程中，我们才会更加了解哪些文献对自己来说最重要。我个人认为文献一般分为三类：第一类是最核心的文献，比如《面向学习的测评：一种系统的方法》就是 LOA 的核心文献之一，还有 Carless、Purpura、Taylor 等的著述显然是 LOA 的核心文献。第二类就是与你的主题比较相关的文献，比如同样以 LOA 为例，与 LOA 相关的其他学者的实证或综述文献，尤其是发表在高水平期刊上的文献。那怎么判断高水平期刊？我觉得 SSCI 期刊应该算是高水平的期刊，比如测试领域的 *Language Testing*、*Language Assessment Quarterly*、*Assessing Writing*，还有应用语言学领域的 *Applied Linguistics*、*TESOL Quarterly*、*System* 等，毫无疑问都是高水平期刊。第三类文献就是有些相关的文献，比如与 LOA 相关的 formative assessment 的文献。

对于这三类文献，我觉得阅读目的不一样，阅读方法也是不一样的。最核心的、最直接相关的文献肯定是要精读的；对于第二类比较相关的，我建议泛读；对于最后一类有些相关的，我建议快速浏览。但最关键的问题还是我们一定要清楚自己想要做什么。据我所知，青年教师，包括学生都比较急，都是想要尽快评职称、尽快毕业，但我觉得这不是读文献的根本目的。我们读文献的根本目的，首先是让自己内心比较安宁。

阅读文献是为了让我们能够更好地做好本职工作。那么怎么去做，刚才 Nick 也讲到了 perseverance，就是恒心、毅力。如果你对某一个话题比较感兴趣，那么我鼓励你第一步应该穷尽性地搜集文献，之后把文献分为这三类，然后从读最核心的文献开始。

关于青年教师是否应该考博，我觉得高校教师，只要可能还是应该读博士。读博士的三五年是你一生当中能够沉静下来、能够系统输入、能够得到专业学术训练的一个过程。这个过程是一种思维的转变，是一种在认识论哲理层面的转变。所以我觉得读博还是很有必要的。

当然，也可能有一部分老师因为各种原因不能选择去读博士。据我所知，有一部分老师因此就放弃了进步，我觉得很不应该。就算不能够读博士，但也一定要学习。如果别人读博士用三五年的时间学习，那么我们自己学习可以用 5 年、10 年，我觉得同样是可以赶上的。我们老一辈的学者，比如杨惠中教授、桂诗春教授等，他们并没有博士学位，但他们的学识是我们这些后辈很难赶上的，因为他们有学术情怀，他们就是终身学习的最好例子。像杨惠中教授已经 80 多岁了，仍然在做学问，在写学术文章。我们不要把自己的学术生命看得那么短。我知道现在有些外界的评价机制对我们有比较大的影响，但是你不要限制自己的学术生命，不要想只有 10 年、20 年，不要想 25 岁、35 岁、45 岁、55 岁的年龄段必须怎么样，你要想着你 85 岁还可以做呢。所以，我觉得读不读博不是最关键的，最关键的是我们要终身学习。

申请读博在国内和国外不太一样。国内读博需要考试，而且导师会比较看重你的科研经历，比如有没有发表的科研成果等。国外读博首先要过语言关，要考雅思、托福等，然后要有很好的 research proposal。

5. 我是一名入职两年的初中英语教师，教学管理一直让我比较头疼，所以想请教您：1）大班化教学，学校处于城乡接合部，学生的学习主动性和积极性不高，考虑到学生每天有大量的作业和课程，该如何有效地要求学生，进而促进学生学习呢？2）严师出高徒，想跟您请教您平时是如何落实对学生的严格要求的？

辜向东：

我想我们作为老师最重要的：第一，就是一定要相信学生是可教的。如果没有这个基本的认识，教学就会很难；第二，就是要去尝试教的方法。比如，我们每天能不能有那么一个小时左右的时间放开，让孩子自己选择阅读，我们提供可供选择的材料。我们可以建一个小型的图书馆、资料室或者电子阅览室，学生可以去看，去浏览。学生的学习主动性和积极性不高是有原因的，因为我们给他们的东西他们不感兴趣。我想我们总是能够找到对学生有吸引力的英文阅读材料。

关于对学生的要求，我觉得学生还没有形成自觉自律之前，就是要硬性规定任务。比如，我现在的研一学生，就是在群里帮助整理文献的三位，我对她们的要求是一周中 5 天必须每天读一篇高水平文献，而且要写读书笔记，然后周日发给我。她们的读书笔记和周记可详可略，但是一定要发给我，这样我就可以监测她们的学习过程，也会给一些简短的反馈。另外，只要我在校，我都会争取每周给她们一次面对面的指导。现在她们已经阅读了上百篇文献，相当不错，我已经能够感受到每一个学生都有了长足的进步。

另外，我对学生的训练可能不只是学术的，更多的是考虑他们很多 universal virtues 的培养，比如我提到的"剑桥人生胜任力框架"（Cambridge Life Competencies Framework）的六种能力（creative thinking, critical thinking, learning to learn, communication, collaboration and social responsibility），我都希望在学术指导的过程当中嵌入进去培养。例如 social responsibility，这一次我们导读能够这么顺利地开展，跟她们三位的奉献是有关系的，但也是在我的提示或提醒之下她们才努力去做的。在这个过程当中，她们去做了，就一定会有收获，而且她们去分享了，就会感受到自己实际上是在帮助建立一个 academic community。

提到 community，我们老师或学生一定要想办法去建立自己的 academic community。每一个人都需要很多不同的 community，在一个 community 当中，每一个人都要想到我能为 community 做什么，然后别人才可能在你需要帮助的时候帮助你。

6. 请您推荐一些适合非英语专业学生的阅读材料，可以从哪里搜集？比如您提到的 CNN，手机 App 好像下载不了英文版。

辜向东：

这个太多了，我就给你推荐两个。一个就是我前面提到的"蔡雷英语"，这个公众号每天都有更新，各个年龄段的学习材料都有。另外一个是"英文巴士"微信公众号，也是每天都有更新，上面的材料都是原汁原味的语言材料。我刚才提到这个 CNN，苹果手机可以下载 APP。当然肯定还有很多其他材料，平时我们老师要用好这些资源。很多微信公众号都在分享，你要去浏览、跟踪。其实看手机上的信息也可以训练快速阅读的能力和快速捕捉有用信息的能力。

7. 1）作为教师，我们在平时的教学中如何去实施测试来辅助教学。在平时的教学中我喜欢用一些小测试，检验学生所学的知识，口头的比较多。现在我们上网课，测试的频率可以比线下多，形式比线下丰富，并且能够快速得到结果的直观呈现。那么我们如何才能对这些结果进行有效的分析和解读？ 2）您在教学方面做过什么样的测试，哪些测试活动您认为是比较有效的；测试完成后，我们需要做些什么，您能不能跟我们说一说？ 3）目前我在对学生进行英语专业四级的阅读和完形填空的训练。那么我怎么从英语专业四级测试入手，来进行一些相关的研究呢？

辜向东：

第一个关于在平时教学当中如何实施测试来辅助教学，我随便举几个很简单的例子。因为我最近做了一些尝试，我也教过大二的非英语专业和英语专业的学生。我做过一些很简单的任务的尝试。我也问过一些中学老师，中学老师经常抱怨说学生连标点符号怎么使用都不知道。我就问，你有没有跟他们做过标点符号使用的训练？其中的设计很简单，找几篇适合学生水平的原汁原味的英文文章，把标点符号全部去掉，让学生去打标点符号。通过实践就能够培养起学生标点符号使用的意识，英文的标点符号使用跟中文是不一样的，不是一逗到底。再比如说，我们都知道学生学习时态和介词用法总是很困难，包括我们自己也一样，冠词用法到现在也搞不清楚。但是我们从来没有做过这种训练，比如把文章当中的冠词全部去掉，让学生去填。我们教材的课文都可以这样做，但是我们其实很少用这种练习去做，而这种东西不需要我们大量批改，只需要让学生去对原文就好了。这样的测试就可以很好地帮助我们的教学。

后面两个问题，我建议可以先去收集文献，也可以从我们团队的文献开始。我们团队做了很多大学英语四、六级，英语专业四、八级，高考以及教学方面的研究，各个层次的都有，其实还是回到一个原点的问题，就是我们要有足够的学术甚至非学术的输入。

8. 作为一位非测试研究方向的外语教师，需要了解多少相关知识比较有利于实际的英语教学呢？既然已经看了一些相关文献，如果要写测试学或者教学类的学术论文，是不是必须要会用 SPSS 等软件进行数据分析，投稿才有希望？

辜向东：

作为外语老师，到底对测试学的知识要了解多少才能够对我们的教学比较有帮助，我认为：第一，其实我们作为一线教师，不管你的研究方向是什么，可能都或多或少需要了解测试学的一些知识，因为教学和测试永远是相生相伴的。第二，我们的研究方向与教学是不矛盾的。比如，我就一直希望有一个做文学研究的人能跟我一起来做文学的测试研究。不管是英语专业还是非英语专业，学生的文学素养怎么去测？这两者不可以结合起来吗？而且最近些年，我看到越来越多的研究者用应用语言学的方法做文学研究。现在国内国外都有很多这方面的尝试，我建议也可以找来看一看，开拓文学研究的这个路径。我今天也说了，Bachman本科就是学文学出身的，他也是后来因为工作需要开始测试研究与实践，后来读博士时做的测试学的研究。

第二个问题，写测试学或者教学类的学术论文是不是必须要会用 SPSS 的软件进行数据分析后，投稿才有希望，这个不一定。在国际期刊的文献当中，如果我估计没错的话，有 1/3，甚至可能超过 1/3 的文献不是定量的研究，定性的研究也很多的。但是我感觉定性的研究对研究者深入研究文献的能力要求特别高，而且对于自己学科领域文献的掌握和阐释能力要非常强。我们国内也有，基本上每一个期刊可以说都发表过定性研究的文章，只是相对来说定性研究要少一些。不过，我觉得我们老师对于方法性的，比如这种定量方法不要太排斥。SPSS 是很简单的，就像我们学开车，学之前觉得很难，但是要把它当作一种工具去学，其实也不是想象那么难，而且这个东西要在用当中去学会比较快一点，因为现在也有一些在线调查，比如问卷星之类的，都可以自动统计。关键的问题是你要研究什么，要对数据能够进行解释。另外，我们虽然在研究方法上欠缺一些，但是可以合作。我在统计学方面也是非常差的，所以我就培养了一些学生，或者是团队里面有善于统计的，我就向他们请教或跟他们合作。现在看来，怎么样能够与更多的人进行合作研究，也是现代社会很重要的一种能力和素质。

9. 1）怎么解决 SSCI 期刊发表文章时的语言问题，像 native speaker 一样学术写作？2）语言测试博士毕业后如果去国外（譬如英国）长期居住，能从事什么样的工作？可以继续做博士后吗？该怎么准备？

辜向东：

积累就是最好的学术写作。我觉得第一步肯定是要看 SSCI 期刊上的文章，看别人的语言是怎么表述的，其实你去看 SSCI 很多文章也是 non-native speakers 写的。第二，无论怎样，我们都是 non-native speakers，所以语言肯定一直都是我们的 bottleneck。现在也有很多的 native speaker 提供这方面的付费审校服务，可能是解决语言问题有效的途径之一。如果你运气好，会找到一些 native speaker 的朋友，他们可以帮助你一起做这个 proofreading，我在想我们高校是不缺这方面的外教或者留学生的。

第二个问题应该是属于少数的。我们也有国内培养的博士，到国外做得很成功的，比如金艳教授的一个博士范劲松，现在在澳大利亚做研究员非常成功，在测试界应该是一个新星。我建议国内读了博士的，如果你希望到国外去工作或者居住的话，第一步最好是申请去做博士后。做博士后有很多的途径，我们国家留学基金委也鼓励博士毕业三年之内，年龄在 35 岁以下的老师去申请国家留学基金委的奖学金。此外，国外也有很多博士后的 vacancy 是提供奖学金的。你出去做两三年博士后，去感受一下是不是适合在国外环境工作，包括在国外环境生活。我在剑桥快十年了，就是去做过一年的访学，后来每年去待两三个月。他们的工作强度我自己真的是承受不了的，你们可以想象，你们觉得我应该算是工作狂了吧。

关于怎么样去准备，我觉得你一定要首先定国家，然后定学校和导师。当然，这些都要根据你自己的能力和研究兴趣去找匹配的导师。在国外，他们更看重的不一定是学校，可能更看重导师；我们国内更看重学校，然后再说导师，各有利弊。当然了，如果你既能找到好学校又能找到好导师，那就再好不过了。我觉得导师的锁定可以从那些终身成就奖获得者、最佳著作奖获得者、论文奖获得者，或者最近几年哪些在这个领域的影响大或者是影响越来越大的学者。这个有的时候也是一种机缘。

除了跟踪学术期刊，就是学术著作。我非常鼓励大家多去参加国内国外的学术会议。当我们见过那些大人物，再回来读他们的著述，就会觉得像在跟他们对话一样。我就这样见过了 Lyle F. Bachman、Alan Davies、Roger Hawkey 等学者，回来再读他们的著述，就像跟他们在对话一样，而且觉得他们其实离我并不遥远。

再扩展性地讲一讲怎么去参加学术会议。我觉得不论是国内还是国外，要出去参加一次会议都是很不容易的，要做一些准备，尤其是当你对这个领域不是那么了解的情况下。我建议要先认真去了解 programs，然后去收集 keynote speakers 的文献，在 parallel sessions 要选出你自己感兴趣的 topics，然后去交流。参加会议过程当中一定要 active，其实很多的交流是在 presentation 之后，所以一定要主动去跟别人交流，你会发现很多 peers 其实跟你是在同一个 stage。这样就可以开始建立你的 academic community。当然，如果你有很好的准备，也可以向那些大咖提问，去走近他们。真正的学者，他们都是愿意跟同辈和年轻人交流的。

10. 我想请问您，处于半放养状态的研究生怎样利用三年时间提升自己呢？想为读博士作准备，我感觉自己拥有了太多自由，而不知道怎么安排自己，怎样能够多多积累 evidence of learning 呢？我在学校也旁听学术会议、认真上课，但是感觉自己没有方向。

辜向东：

其实我们导师是很难的，对学生抓得太紧，觉得给他们成长的自由度不够，抓得不紧吧，学生还觉得你太放任，或者老师觉得能不能这样放任学生，其实各有利弊。我发觉我平时对学生抓得这么紧，但我的学生完成任务，比如每年到硕士论文那个阶段，我的学生都不如其他老师的学生完成得那么快、那么早。

导师管与不管确实有一个度。我觉得其实半放养状态是最理想的，就是老师管一部分，也放一部分。我自己经常在想这个度怎么去把握，这就是围城效应，因为你管得太多了，学生就觉得没有自己成长的空间和时间，你不管了，他又觉得你放任。你才研一就能这么积极主动地参与这样的导读活动，而且一直在积极地分享自己的收获和思考等，这都是很好的。只要你想学，总是能够找到志同道合的，甚至也可能找到愿意指导你的老师。

我想你首先可能需要尽早明确要不要读博，接下来就是去做。比如说，你现在很明确要读博士，你这三年就一定要多参加学术会议，不管有没有会议发言都要多去参加。你们广外每年举办那么多的学术会议，不管跟自己领域相不相关，都尽可能去听，多去接触那些国内外的学者。说不定这个过程当中就能遇到你的导师，我认识 Bachman 就是在读博士期间参加学术会议，听到他的发言，跟他提一些问题，然后陪他参观东方明珠。后来我就提出想去他那里做访问学者，他就说我必须要有博士学位。所以，我博士毕业之后拿到了学校的奖学金，就去了他那里做访学，访学回来这么多年也一直跟他断断续续保持联系。后来我去剑桥也得到他的强力推荐，国外是非常看重推荐的。我的意思是，即使你没有机会，都要创造机会，更何况你们现在的年轻人都有很多的机会，一定要珍惜机会。

其次，要尝试写一些学术文章。学术文章肯定是要在大量的输入和思考的基础上。如果没有好的选题，也可以去找人帮助，包括你的导师、你认识的人，也包括我，我可以给你提供一些选题去思考，然后指导你，或者合作。这些都是可能的，更多的导师也是可能的。

11. 辜老师您的百人计划大概什么时候开始，可以透露更多相关内容吗？

辜向东：

我这个想法是在 2019 年底产生的。我想我未来可能还能工作十年。我学术上是做不到那种大咖级的，但是我还是比较善于培养人才，尤其是从零起步培养他们上路，然后有望他们去成为大咖。而且，最近五年到十年间我在国内外都有讲座、讲学，觉得有一批青年教师和学生很需要成长的指导，mentoring 和 tutoring 是我们非常需要加强的。我为什么会产生这个想法呢？因为我儿子是2009 年上的大学，到 2019 年，正好是十年。这十年我看到了他的成长，也看到了我的一批学生的成长。我最近几年也指导了一些中学和高校青年教师，培养他们从零起步到在一般期刊发表文章，然后在国际期刊发表文章，再到申请国外读博或考上国内博士，等等。所以，2020 年一开始，外研社李老师邀请我做第 66期"我来读文献"的导读，我就想起我的百人计划，觉得这真是天赐良缘。所以，这一期导读，我就要把它做成百人计划的起步。这两个微信群差不多 1000 人，有一批老师和学生从头跟到尾，就无意当中成了百人计划的候选人，所以我会从他们开始边做边尝试。我很希望能够有更多的人加入，来一起做这个事儿，而且我很希望能够传帮带，比如我指导博士生，博士生指导硕士生，硕士生指导本科生。我总是觉得，一个人可能走得很快，但是一群人才能走得更远。

12. 我是重大校友，后来在墨尔本读了语言测试学硕士，现在从事本科英语教学。我从去年起对系统功能语言学产生了很大的兴趣，想找到 SFL 和语言测试（尤其是写作方面）的结合点，请您给一些建议。

辜向东：

如果你对写作测试或者写作感兴趣的话，我推荐两个期刊，一个是 *Assessing Writing*，另一个是 *The Second Language Writing*。这两个期刊，如果你能够跟踪五到十年的文献，你会发现哪些学者的著作值得关注，这样你就能够找到你的 interface。当然你肯定应该已经知道系统功能语言学这个领域国内外有哪些人物、哪些学者是领军学者，应该去关注他们的文献。关于怎么样去了解自己领域哪些学者是有影响的学者，我觉得任何一个学科领域都一定会有学术团体。比如，我们语言测试界就有 the International Language Testing Association，ILTA 的年会叫 Language Testing Research Colloquium，这是我们领域最高级别的会议。我们也有其他的会议，比如欧洲语言测试协会的会议、亚洲语言测试者协会的会议，教师也有 TESOL、IATEFL、Asia TEFL 这些会议，我建议大家去关注这些学会和学术会议。然后，你可以从 keynote speakers 以及他们相应的学术期刊开始，比如国际语言测试协会的期刊就是 *Language Testing*，后来有 *Language Assessment Quarterly*，*Assessing Writing*，当然还有教育测量的期刊等。所以，一定要去关注这些领域的学者、顶级的期刊、学会的年会等。我是 2008 年第一次参加测试领域最高级别的会议 Language Testing Research Colloquium。当时是何莲珍教授第一次把这个会议引进在中国召开，而且当时已经是第 30 届，我当时是自费前往。我鼓励老师多去自费参加学术会议，因为如果是自费的话，你就会懂得珍惜。我当时就是从那次会议开始，把能够找到的过去 30 年的会议 programs 全部下载并打印出来。2008 年那个暑假，我读了这些 programs，然后下决心从此以后要跟踪这个会议，从 2009 年开始向这个会议投摘要。我们团队今年在这个会议有三篇文章入选。这个会议本来今年应该在非洲的突尼斯召开，现在推迟了。

13. 能否推荐一下 SSCI 上写得比较好的综述类论文？

辜向东：

我推荐 *Annual Review of Applied Linguistics*，上面每一篇文章都是综述文章，而且作者都是在那个领域有影响的人。另外，推荐大家关注 SSCI 期刊上的，尤其是跟自己相关领域的 SSCI 期刊上的 Special Issues，上面一定会有一两篇综述类文章。

14. 我在阅读杨惠中老师的"创建中国特色大学英语测试系统的风雨历程"一文的时候，文章说为保证考试的信度和效度达到教育测量学的要求，要在考前就获得试题难易度、区分度等数据。如何在考前获得这些数据呢？我们每年期末考试后也要根据成绩对试卷做分析，里面也有难易度和区分度两个数据。但同一套卷子不同的班级得出的难易度和区分度是不一样的，并且是根据考后成绩得出的，那四、六级考试试卷的难易度和区分度怎么在考前就得出呢？并且对于不同的群体这个难易度和区分度不是也会不一样吗？

辜向东：

凡是大规模高风险考试，正式实施之前，客观性题目都是要做试测的，而且都要获得测试题目的难易度、区分度等数据，然后才能投入使用，因为大规模高风险考试的标准化要求非常高。而我们的校本考试，尤其是期末考试，对老师的专业化程度和考试本身的要求可能没那么高。难易度、区分度都是老师个人在掌握，最好还是应该有一个团队来做 expert judgement。我们很难去做试测，但实际上我们如果有一个团队，我们也可以由老师来做试测。

我个人曾经参加过重庆市的高考命题。我们的高考命题出来以后，都要有几个老师专门来做这个题，而且老师要做 expert judgement，要判断它的这个难度和区分度。然后，再找一些各个水平段选出来的受试来做试测，之后再修改，最后才能用到正式的高考当中。其他的大规模高风险考试也是一样的。至于你说的，我们虽然是考试之后再做试卷分析，分析当然也是很有必要的，其实考试前和考试后都应该做这种分析。另外，对于同一套试卷，不同的班级的难易度、区分度是不一样的，因为学生的水平不同。大部分高风险考试跟校本考试虽然有很多不同，但我们都要努力去追求信度和效度，因为即便是校本考试，对学生个体也是有影响的。当然，有的影响是决定性的，有的影响可能要小一些。

在校本考试当中，越来越强调公平性。所以我们在考试，包括形成性评价的过程当中，确定标准是非常重要的。标准包括评分的标准，包括我们评定 evidence 的标准。就是我们对学生 performance 的抽样的 size、coverage，都应该属于我们考虑的范围。可能更多地还是需要去看一些入门的期刊文献和专著。我跟大家推荐一本书：*Language Testing for Teachers*。这是一本比较早的，专门针对老师的语言测试书，是英文版的，我觉得现在都还很实用。另外，我的微信公众号"人生 GU 事"曾经推送过一个"我们一起学测试"的系列，大家可以去看一看。

15. 学校的期末考试（校本考试）会出现教学大纲和考试大纲脱节的问题，据我了解，很多学校是没有考试大纲的，请问这个问题在教学中怎么解决？

辜向东：

这是一个非常普遍的问题。我觉得我们老师一定要钻研大纲，大学英语现在叫"课程标准"，英语专业叫"国标"，而且要去看课标、国标本身，也要去看设计这些国标和课程标准的学者的著述和阐释，然后在教学当中去执行大纲，考试要以大纲为准。当然，我所知道的有些学校已经有所谓的 proficiency test，也是一种探索。校本考试也是很好的一种探索，里面也有很多值得研究的问题。

在国际上，很多人非常关注这个 classroom assessment、school-based assessment，在国内我们还是更关注 large scale assessment，不过倾向会慢慢地改变。但是我们是一线老师，可能要非常关注怎么样去提升对期末考试的试卷、平时学生成绩的评定，以及课堂的教学质量和在课堂中如何有效地使用测试等。

16. 请问您对高职层次的测试，特别是高职职业英语的测试感兴趣吗？我在实际工作中，感到高职学生没有贴合的测试，对他们的学习动机形成很不利。

辜向东：

国际上非常关注 vocational education，也有相关的一些测试，比如剑桥的医护英语考试、剑桥商务英语考试，应该还有更多的这类考试。我觉得不论是哪一种级别、哪一种类型的考试，就像 LOA 书上讲的，所有的测试都有一些 basic components，我们可以把那些 basic components 作为标准，考察是否符合。

17. 不同层次的学校和不同层次的学生，考试收集的数据不一样，那校本考试和《中国英语能力等级量表》怎么对接？

辜向东：

《中国英语能力等级量表》一个很好的功能是给我们提供了一个统一的度量。我们可以将不同的考试、不同水平的学生对接到这个度量上。所以这个量表出来以后，其实不应该一对一地对应到相应的 educational stage，因为在同一个 educational stage 大家的英语水平可能差异也会很大，真正对应的是学生的水平，而不是这个 educational stage。有个性和共性的东西，可能是我们对相关的文献输入比较少。比如，关于与《中国英语能力等级量》的对接，我觉得应该先去看关于它的研发。现在也已经有一些实证研究的文献，我们团队已经有三篇，我也在群里分享了的。关于 CEFR 应用研究的文献就更多了，所以我们还是要从文献输入开始。这可能是一个普遍的问题,输入需要极大地加强,而且需要持续地加强。

关于英语能力提升,我觉得一线教师,包括学生,提升语言水平是第一要务。最近几年我才意识到,其实这个应该是从一开始学习语言就一定要重视。我现在主张通过培养学生的学术能力的同时培养他们的语言水平。比如 APA 格式规范,学生读英文的同时就学了规范,但是我们的教学当中一直都欠缺这些东西。学的语言其实是很空的,没有什么思想内容,知识面也没有扩充,即使投入了很多的时间和精力,也难以真正地提高水平、提升能力。另外要考虑选择材料的思想性和内容性,内容要引导学生去延伸思考。比如很多国家和地区领导人关于一些时事的发言文本,都是真实的,而且与我们紧密相关,对于我们自己和学生来说也是很好的学习材料。读了之后去思考对我们个体,对机构团体、对一个国家、对全社会,甚至全世界的影响,培养他们的国际视野、人文情怀等综合素质。

18. 我十分关注且有意愿参与所在省市高中英语教师的测试研课坊,团队成员包括省教育考试院老师、教研员和一线教师,但有点不确定如何准备合适的阅读材料。

辜向东:

我非常推荐 British Council 和 Cambridge English 的网站,当然包括 ETS,上面有很多现成的关于做师资培训的材料。我们国内也有些机构的微信公众号推荐在不断地更新,大家可以关注。现在也有很多免费的课程,比如我今天看到 Cambridge Assessment English 就在推出一系列的关于慕课的限时免费课程资源。另外,LOA 学习是社会性的,我建议一定要建立学习共同体,大家一起探讨,共同提高。